THE COMPLETE ITALIAN COOKBOOK

THE COMPLETE ITALIAN COOKBOOK

With more than 250 authentic and
easy-to-follow recipes illustrated in full color

edited by Diana Vowles

SHOOTING STAR PRESS

A QUANTUM BOOK

Published by Shooting Star Press, Inc.
230 Fifth Avenue, Suite 1212
New York, NY 10001
USA

This edition printed 1996

ISBN 1-57335-528-3

This book was produced by
Quantum Books Ltd
6 Blundell Street
London N7 9BH

Printed in China by Leefung-Asco Printers Ltd

The material in this publication previously appeared in
The Flavors of Italy, *Italian Trattoria Cooking*, *Cooking with Pasta*
and *The Pasta and Pizza Cookbook*

CONTENTS

The artist Longlin's depiction of a sumptuous 18th-century banquet, held in Venice in honor of the visiting Elector of Cologne.

The Origins Of Italian Cooking

The cooking of Italy is the mother of all European cuisine, a fact acknowledged by even the 'Larousse Gastronomique'. Its origins are well recorded by the writers of ancient Rome, who have left very vivid impressions of the orgies indulged in by the ruling classes — but this is only half the picture.

While the aristocracy sat down, or rather reclined, to such dishes as peacock dressed in all its feathers or boar stuffed with live thrushes, the common soldier was roasting his ration of millet on a stone set in the campfire. When it was done, he crushed it, boiled it up with water and ate it as gruel. What was left over solidified into a cake and was consumed cold. This primitive meal was called *pulmentum*, and it has survived right up to the present day in the tastier form of polenta, whereas the more excessive dishes of the Empire, though more memorable, declined and fell with it.

Though what endured was, like polenta, deeply rooted in peasant life, the extravagance of Imperial tables is impossible to ignore. Flamingos and herons were also served up in their plumage; hedgehogs, puppies, wolves and donkeys enjoyed a great popularity; dormice were kept in a barrel to stop them losing weight by exercise and were fed until they were fat, then roasted in honey and herbs. A favorite banquet recipe was "Trojan pork." The title referred to the horse of Troy, which had concealed the ambushing Greek soldiers. Trojan pork was stuffed with oysters and songbirds. One side of it was smeared with meal soaked in wine and oil and roasted, then the pig was turned over and the uncooked side was dipped into boiling water until it was done. Among the more exotic delicacies of the day were camel's foot and elephant's trunk.

All these things were consumed in stupendous quantities by the few who could afford them. The Emperor Maximinius is reputed to have eaten over 40lb of meat a day, and to have drunk 35pt of wine. The Emperor Aurelian commissioned an actor, Farone, to amuse him by eating in one session a whole sheep, a whole sucking pig and a whole boar, accompanied by 100 buns and 100 bottles of wine.

The ancient Romans were fond of cooking with all the herbs and spices to which their vast empire gave them access. The original Roman seasoning was salt, evaporated from the water at the mouth of the river Tiber. It was used as a preservative for meat, and when more was made than could be used at home it became the basis for Rome's first important export trade, carried out of the city along the via Salaria – the Salt Road – which remains to this day.

To make salted meat more palatable, the Romans later added honey, dried fruit and spices. The resulting taste was the ancestor of today's *agrodolce*, a bittersweet sauce enjoyed with many different foods, including game and cabbage. A less attractive flavoring that seems to have been used liberally to disguise the taste of salt meat was *garum*, which one writer described as a sauce made from the entrails of mackerel.

Poultry could be reared by every household and there was a plentiful supply of chickens from Roman markets. Guinea fowl, squab and duck were also popular, and when the Romans conquered Gaul they discovered a great liking for goose. Consequently the returning troops drove huge flocks of geese from Picardy to Rome, living off the fields and causing much devastation as they went.

During the 2nd century the Emperor Trajan built the Forum, and next to it on Quirinal Hill a supermarket, a semi-circular structure with both open-air and closed booths. Behind it rambled multi-storey buildings housing more shops and stalls. There the Romans bought and sold meat and poultry, fish and wine. Olive oil was imported from Spain, wheat from Egypt and spices from Asia.

Cabbage was grown by the better-off, while the poor ate beans, mallow and a species of nettle. Spinach was not known till the 9th century, when it was introduced from Persia. Persia also provided Italy with melons, which farmers began to cultivate at Cantalupo, outside Rome. Figs and wild cherries were highly-prized natives.

Honey was used as a sweetener – even on savory foods. The Roman dish of honeyed eggs, *ova mellita*, gave its name to today's omelet. Another food given the sweet treatment was cheese. Flour and crushed fresh cheese were mixed with honey and eggs and baked in an earthenware mold – the cheesecake was born. The crushed fresh cheese in question was the ancestor of ricotta, but the Romans had a dozen varieties of cheese, of which they were very fond.

In the 3rd century AD Rome fell to the barbarians and the excesses of the degenerate empire were replaced by a more sober lifestyle. Recipes were preserved, as were other writings, in monasteries. In the 9th century came the Islamic invasion, which brought a new injection of life into Italian cooking. The Arabs brought with them the techniques of making ice cream and sorbet, and introduced desserts and sweet cakes made with marzipan. They were also responsible for planting the first sugar cane in Europe, but its cultivation did not really catch on until 200 years later, when cane and refined sugar were brought back by the Crusaders. Sugar went under the name of "Indian salt" and was used as salt was, to season fish and meat. The Crusaders also reintroduced the spices that had been known in the days of ancient Rome, and a new interest in cooking sprang up. Milk and egg pies, vegetable tarts and bread sweetened with dried fruit appeared in a recipe book around 1290, along with the first-ever mention of pasta.

When Marco Polo opened up the spice trade between Venice and the Far East, Venetians grew fat on the profits and Venice became a center of gastronomy. It was there that the table fork became popular and that drinking vessels were first made of fine glass.

In 16th century Florence the first modern cooking academy was set up. Called *Compagnia del Paiolo* (Company of the Cauldron), one of its members was the painter Andrea del Sarto, who presented his colleagues with an exhibition dish made of gelatine in the shape of a temple held up by pillars of sausages and parmesan. Inside was a book with pages of pasta, and in front stood roasted thrushes, singing notes inscribed on the pasta in peppercorns.

In 1533 Catherine de Medici journeyed from Florence to France to marry the future King Henri II. France was still in the dark ages as far as the art of cooking was concerned, and Catherine took with her her own chefs and pastrycooks, who were adept at making ices, cakes and cream puffs. Marie de Medici followed in her footsteps in 1600 to become the bride of Henri IV. The Florentines were responsible for introducing haricot beans, petit pois, broccoli, artichokes and leafy cabbage to the French, and they also educated them in the culinary skills that were soon to make their own cuisine great and renowned the world over.

From Italy too came the double boiler. The French adopted it as the *bain marie*, but the original Mary's bath or *bagno maria* was named after its inventor Maria de Cleofsa, an alchemist who devised it to help her with her arcane researches into the relationship between magic, medicine and cooking.

The 16th century saw the arrival of the first tomato in Italy, brought back to Europe with the first red pepper from Mexico by the Spanish conquistadors. Called the *pomo d'oro* (golden apple), it was a cherry-sized yellow fruit used as a salad vegetable. It took 200 years for the large luscious red varieties to be developed for use in cooking.

Coffee was imported from the East. In 1585 Venice's ambassador to Turkey described to the Senate "the habit of the Turks of drinking a black water as hot as you can bear it, taken from seeds called *cavee*, and they say it has the power of keeping men awake." Its popularity was quickly established in Venice and soon spread all over Europe.

The arrival of the potato was greeted with less enthusiasm. Pope Clement VII's botanist classified the specimen presented to him as "a small truffle" and thenceforward it was cultivated in Italian gardens – as a decorative plant. The Italians were not alone in their confusion as to what to do with the potato – Queen Elizabeth I's chef threw away the tubers and served up the leaves. Potatoes never became a staple in Italy, even when their true use was discovered. Corn, the last major import, which came from America, provided a more popular alternative form of starch.

By the 16th century the French had become so advanced in the art of cooking that chefs from the French court were sent back to Venice to demonstrate their skills. The Venetians were not impressed. "French cooks have ruined the Venetian stomach," wrote Gerolamo Zanetti, "with so much porchere (filth) . . . sauces, broths, extracts . . . garlic and onion in every dish . . . meat and fish transformed to such a point that they are scarcely recognizable by the time they get to the table . . . Everything mashed and mixed up with a hundred herbs, spices, sauces . . ."

Though the author was a biased (Venetian) observer writing some 400 years ago, his comment serves to underline the major difference between present-day Italian and French cooking. For while French cuisine tends to be elaborate and subtle, that of Italy is bold, simple and direct. Zanetti's mistrust of foreigners' meddling with good basic ingredients, transforming them into something "scarcely recognizable," also shows a fierce respect for local tradition that is very much part of Italian cooking today. It is not just influence from abroad that is resisted, but influence from other regions of Italy, and it is this that makes Italian cooking so varied and so unique.

Outside Florence in the evening, the time of day all Florentines settle down to their evening meal. Florentines eat well but simply, disdaining the complicated sauces and seasonings of other regions.

The harbor at Sorrento, where fish fresh from the sea is the local specialty.

THE FLAVORS OF ITALY

Italian cooking is the cooking of its regions. Until 1861 the regions of Italy were separate and often hostile states. Geographically as well as politically isolated from each other, the regions developed their own distinctive culinary character and traditions, traditions that are fiercely and proudly preserved today.

In Italy what is local is best. An Emilian would regard a salami produced in neighbouring Tuscany with scepticism; a Tuscan might smile ruefully at the Emilian's extravagant use of butter and cream. It follows that the traveler intent on enjoying Italian food should always order what the locals eat. It is no good asking for osso buco in Naples or beefsteak in Genoa, because they will be but pale imitations of the genuine things to be had in Milan and Florence – and you will have missed the opportunity to sample the perfect spaghetti alla marinara and torta pasqualina.

Italian pride in local fare and disdain of "imports," be they from only a few miles away, is soundly rooted in a love of fresh food. If there is one aspect of cooking shared by all the regions of Italy, it is the importance placed on the quality of the ingredients. Fruit and vegetables must be home-grown, preferably without chemical fertilizers, and picked at the peak of ripeness and glossy perfection. A squeeze of lemon juice is known to have more zest when the lemon is freshly picked from the tree and still warm from the sun, than when it has traveled long distances, ripening slowly in a crate. Meat should be home-reared and home-killed, and fish straight from the catch – seafood is rarely served at any distance from the coast.

All over Italy, Italians treat their food with respect. Their cooking is designed to emphasize the natural flavors of the ingredients. In this it is very different from French cooking, with its subtle harmonies and sophisticated sauces. Italian food is brightly colored when it reappears on the plate. It is good, wholesome, hearty and endlessly varied – essentially home cooking that requires very few skills to master.

The main meal in Italy is eaten in the middle of the day and can consist of several courses. First there may be a soup. This is usually a clear broth made substantial with rice or pasta, shredded vegetables or the dumplings made of potato or semolina called gnocchi. An alternative to soup would be a risotto or a dish of baked or boiled pasta with a piquant or creamy sauce. Generous helpings of freshly grated Parmesan cheese top this first course. Next comes a dish of fish or meat. In some areas the meat would be quite plainly cooked, perhaps broiled with aromatic olive oil and herbs as its only added flavoring; in others it might be a more complicated dish layered with melting cheese and tender ham coated in breadcrumbs and fired in pork fat until succulent and golden.

A *contorno* – literally a contour – of seasonal vegetables or salad can be served with or after this course. To finish with, there will be fruit and local cheese, and the meal is of course accompanied by the wine of the region.

On Sundays or special occasions lunch may begin with antipasti – a selection of salami, fish, olives, artichokes and other savory appetizers both hot and cold – and end with one of Italy's famous desserts, ices, cakes or pastries and black espresso coffee and liqueurs.

The foodshops of Bologna, which is renowned as the gastronomic capital of Italy, are Aladdin's caves for the gourmet. A dazzling display of sausages, cheeses, mushrooms, preserved fruits and pickled vegetables compete for the shopper's attention.

Lazio, Umbria and the Marches

This central band across the knee of Italy is dominated by the capital, Rome. The Roman appetite is robust and hearty, and the food that satisfies it is both good and simple. Suckling pig stuffed with herbs and roasted on a spit is a typical favorite dish. The Roman gastronomical calendar moves from festival to festival, with roast capon at Christmas, stuffed with breadcrumbs, salami, giblets and cheese; suckling lamb at Easter, and on Midsummer Night, snails in a sauce of garlic, anchovy, tomato and mint.

In Rome you can eat both the fresh homemade pasta of the north, in a justly famous dish of cannelloni – flat pasta sheets rolled around a meat filling – and the dried tubular pasta of the south. Sauces include tuna and mushrooms (alla carrettiera), hot and red peppers (all'arrabbiata – rabid!) and *alla carbonara*, made with salt pork, eggs and cream.

Saltimbocca, the picturesque name meaning "jump in the mouth," is slices of ham atop slices of veal, flavored with sage, fried in butter and then braised in white wine. Straciatella is another well-known dish, a clear soup with a mixture of eggs, flour and cheese poured into it. It breaks up as it cooks, forming the "little rags" that give the soup its name.

For dessert you might be offered zuppa inglese, neither soup nor English, but a rich trifle flavored with rum.

The mountainous region of Umbria is the biggest producer – and hence consumer – of meat in the whole of Italy. There is plenty of game in the higher regions, sheep and goats a little further down and cattle and pigs on the foothills. The pork in particular is excellent. The animals are fattened on acorns and much of the meat is cured and turned into sausages spiced with garlic, pepper, pine nuts and fennel.

Umbria is famed even in France for its superb truffles, eaten sliced on pasta, and for its freshwater fish in particular the roach.

Most of the inhabitants of the Marches lives along the coast, and it follows that fish is the staple of their diet. Each seaside town has its own way of making fish soup, with the ingredients varying according to the day's catch. Snails flavored with fennel, and huge fat olives – stuffed, rolled in breadcrumbs and fried – are other delicacies to be had in the region, while Urbino in the north is distinguished by its sauce. It was first invented by a Duke of Urbino in the 15th century, who was so afraid of being poisoned that he refused to let his chef season his food. Once the food had been tasted for him he added his own sauce, prepared according to a secret recipe by a servant who he trusted.

The recipe was recently rediscovered and the sauce is produced today in a bottle with the Duke's portrait on the label. His profile is disfigured by the removal of the bridge of his nose – a piece of self-inflicted surgery. The Duke's right eye was blinded by the claws of a falcon, and he had the top of his nose cut away so that he could see with his left eye if a would-be assassin was attempting to sneak up on him from the right.

The Regions of Italy

The regions listed below represent the main geographical divisions of Italy. The shields shown are those of the main town or city in each region.

KEY TO REGIONS

LAZIO, UMBRIA AND THE MARCHES
(See left)

TUSCANY
(See p.16)

EMILIA-ROMAGNA
(See p.18)

LIGURIA
(See p.20)

VENETO
(See p.20)

LOMBARDY
(See p.23)

PIEDMONT
(See p.24)

SICILY
(See p.26)

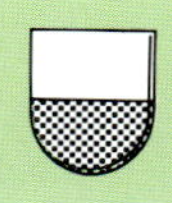

NAPLES AND THE SOUTH: CAMPANIA, CALABRIA, BASILICATA, APULIA AND ABRUZZI-MOLISE
(See p.26)

SARDINIA
(See p.26)

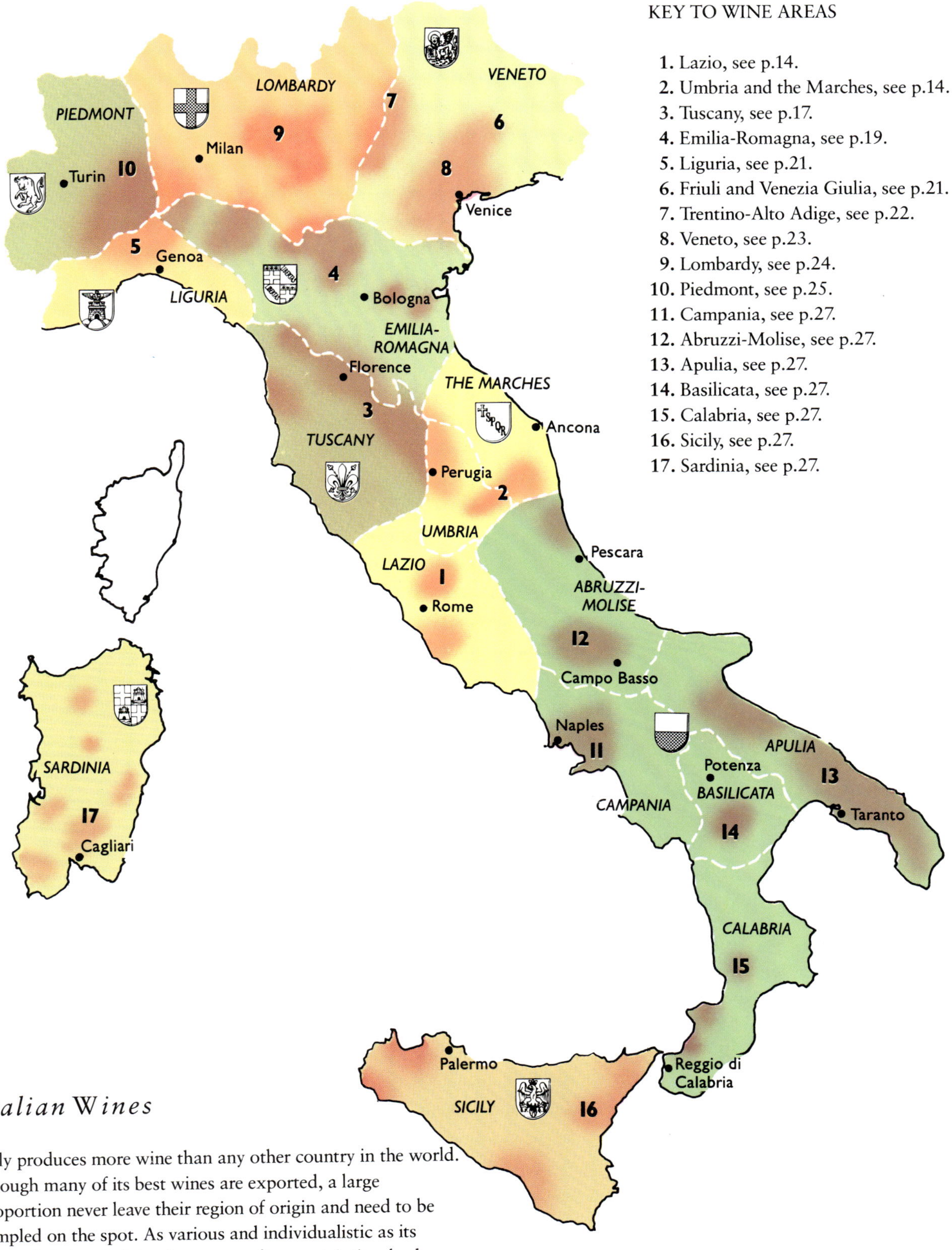

KEY TO WINE AREAS

1. Lazio, see p.14.
2. Umbria and the Marches, see p.14.
3. Tuscany, see p.17.
4. Emilia-Romagna, see p.19.
5. Liguria, see p.21.
6. Friuli and Venezia Giulia, see p.21.
7. Trentino-Alto Adige, see p.22.
8. Veneto, see p.23.
9. Lombardy, see p.24.
10. Piedmont, see p.25.
11. Campania, see p.27.
12. Abruzzi-Molise, see p.27.
13. Apulia, see p.27.
14. Basilicata, see p.27.
15. Calabria, see p.27.
16. Sicily, see p.27.
17. Sardinia, see p.27.

Italian Wines

Italy produces more wine than any other country in the world. Though many of its best wines are exported, a large proportion never leave their region of origin and need to be sampled on the spot. As various and individualistic as its regional dishes, Italy's wines arouse fierce patriotism both locally and internationally.

The Wines of Lazio, Umbria and The Marches

LAZIO

Lazio has two main wine-producing areas: the Castelli Romani in the hills around Rome and the area around Lake Bolsena, about 60 miles from it.

CASTELLI ROMANI

This is an area of 50 sq miles in the Alban hills producing mainly white wine that can be either sweet or dry. The grapes for the sweet wine are allowed to dry out a little on the vine before they are picked and fermented in the caves of the Alban hills. The sweet wines go well with fresh fruit and the dry complement robust Roman pasta dishes and their suckling pigs and baby lambs. The best known of these wines is Frascati, clear gold in color and either dry, semi-sweet or sweet.

CASTELBRACCIANO

A sweet, golden-yellow wine from the shores of Lake Bracciano.

CASTRENSE

Light red and white wines from the shores of Lake Bolsena.

CECUBO

A wine from Gaeta drunk by Cicero and Horace. It is a very light red with a full fragrance.

EST! EST!! EST!!!

There is a curious tale of how this wine came by its name. Local legend has it that an 18th century cardinal on a journey around Italy sent his steward before him to try out the wines in various hostelries. When the steward discovered a good one, he was to chalk Est! ("It is") on the door. At Montefiascone he was so impressed that he chalked Est! Est!! Est!!! before passing out into a stupor. The cardinal arrived and his enthusiasm for the wine was so great that he drank himself to death on it there and then.

UMBRIA AND THE MARCHES

Wine production here is not extensive. The hillsides are very steep and in many cases vines are grown alternating with rows of corn. Both red and white are generally on the rough side, but there are two notable exceptions – Verdicchio dei Castelli di Jesi from the Marches, and Orvieto from Umbria.

ALTE VALLE DEL TENERE

The wines of the upper Tiber, both red and white, are light and simple and ideal for lunchtime drinking.

BIANCHELLO

A light dry white from the Marches, it goes well with fish.

ORVIETO

Made mainly from the Trebbiano grape, this wine has been produced around the cathedral city of Orvieto for at least 500 years. There are two straw-colored whites, one dry and the other semi-sweet. The grapes for the semi-sweet are allowed to begin to rot after they have been picked – in the German Auslese the grapes start to rot on the vine – and the resulting wine is not too sweet to be drunk with fish or poultry. The dry Orvieto is the more popular export.

VERDICCHIO DEI CASTELLI DI JESI

This wine is drunk along the holiday coast around Rimini and is also exported in large quantities. It is one of the very best of the Italian whites, despite the vulgar bottle. Straw-colored and slightly bitter, the best Verdicchio has a secondary fermentation like Chianti.

VIN COTTO

"Cooked wine" is made by reducing must over heat and then topping it up with uncooked must. The wine is fermented and kept for two years. It is strong, rich and sweet.

The Italians' passion for ice cream dates back to the days of the Roman empire, when snow and crushed berries were served at the imperial table.

Tuscany

Tuscany is the heart of Italy. Its food is simply prepared and with the best ingredients. Elaborate dishes have no place on the menu here; indeed the Tuscan way of cooking is sometimes looked upon by outsiders as austere because of its conspicuous lack of complicated sauces and seasonings.

Florence is the capital and, in culinary terms, Florentine (alla fiorentina) is synonymous with spinach. But this is only outside Italy – to an Italian *alla fiorentina* simply means "in the Florentine style." Bistecca alla fiorentina is a typical Tuscan dish well worth traveling miles to sample in its native city – it is simply prepared with ingredients of the highest quality, and it does not contain spinach. Bistecca alla fiorentina is steak from a choice two-year-old Chana Valley bull, grilled, briefly above chestnut wood. It is salted and rubbed with a little olive oil just before it is removed from the fire and served perhaps with fresh beans.

Tuscans are known thoughout Italy as mangiafagioli (bean eaters). They eat beans in soup, beans in risotto and beans with pasta. Beans and tuna fish is a favorite appetizer. Fagioli nel fiasco is beans cooked slowly in a closed flask to prevent the flavor from escaping. They are then eaten simply with olive oil, salt, pepper and lemon juice and Tuscan bread.

The bread in Tuscany is unsalted, as it forms a component part of so many dishes that a too-salty flavor would ruin. There is, for example, a bread salad, tossed with tomatoes, cucumber and pink onions, and a bread and tomato soup, especially beloved by children. The other reason that bread is not salted is that salt absorbs moisture, and bread is bought in big enough quantities to last a week. Salted bread would go moldy before the week was out. The Tuscans are a practical and economy-conscious people.

They are very fond of game, particularly pheasant and hare, which is plentiful in the hillsides, and which they serve simply roasted and flavored with wild rosemary. Their pecorino cheese with its sharp flavor and black crust is one of the best in Italy and is an excellent accompaniment to Chianti, Tuscany's famous wine.

There are two more specialities of the region that deserve a mention – Livorno's splendid fish soup, cacciucco alla livornese, and Siena's flat dessert cake, panforte, full of dried fruit, almonds and spices, often taken home by tourists as a souvenir of the lovely medieval city that makes it.

Pesaro, like all Italian coastal towns, has its own recipe for fish soup, the ingredients for which vary from day to day according to the fishermen's catch.

The Wines of Tuscany

The landscape of Tuscany used to reflect the diet of its inhabitants: bread, olive oil and wine. Corn, olive trees and vines would be grown in the same field, with perhaps a cow or two wandering among them. The peasants had to give half their produce to the landowners and could not risk a single crop. Now the wines have taken over in rows well-spaced enough to allow the passage of a tractor. Still, a few farmers have kept their olive trees, as much because the grey-green color is a vital part of landscape as for their oil.

ARBIA

A dry white wine that goes well with the pecorino – sheep's cheese – of the region. A "virgin" wine, because the must is fermented without stalks or skin.

BRUNELLO DI MONTALCINO

One of the great Italian reds – full and fragrant, smooth and well balanced, it is aged in the cask for five or six years and enthusiasts recommend keeping it in the bottle for up to 50.

CANDIA

Sweet red and white wines from the northwest of the region.

CHIANTI

Baron Bettino Ricasoli "invented" Chianti in the 1860s. When his young wife danced at a ball with a man who seemed to be paying her too much attention, he called her away and they drove all night to Brolio, where there was a gloomy castle the baron's family had not lived in for years. Here they set up a permanent home well away from the temptations of society. The baron diverted himself by developing a new wine – a mixture of black Sangiovese and white Malvasia grapes, and a method of making them ferment twice, giving the wine a novel taste a slight tingle. When the first fermentation is over, a rich must from dried grapes is added to the wine, inducing a second fermentation that lasts from two to three weeks. Wines made by this method are drunk young and sold in typical Chianti flasks covered in wicker (or plastic). Finer Chiantis meant to be aged are only fermented once and sold in ordinary claret bottles. Chianti is produced and exported on a very large scale, but Chianti classico comes only from the area between Florence and Siena and bears the growers' label of a black cockerel against a gold background.

MOSCADELLO DI MONTALCINO

A light, golden fragrant wine with a slight tingle, drunk young and chilled.

UGOLINO BIANCO

A clear straw-colored white from near Livorno. To be drunk young and chilled with fish.

VAL DI CHIANA

A clear, golden-yellow wine, a "virgin" like Arbia, see above left.

VERNACCIA DI SAN GIMIGNANO

A fresh, straw-colored wine with a hint of bitterness comes from around this picturesque town, which has been completely overtaken by tourism. It is a fine, dry white that improves with age.

VIN NOBILE DI MONTEPULCIANO

A smooth, well-balanced ruby red wine with a hint of violet, best after at least five years in the bottle.

VIN SANTO

A rich, sweet dessert wine, very popular in Tuscany.

Emilia-Romagna

This rich and fertile region lying to the north of Tuscany is Italy's land of plenty, and not for nothing is its capital, Bologna, known as *Bologna la grassa* – "The fat." Bologna is the home of mortadella, perhaps Italy's finest sausage, and, above all, fresh pasta. Made from local wheat milled very fine, Bolognese pasta is rolled out so thinly you can almost see through it, cut into long narrow strips to make tagliatelle and served with a tasty ragu, which comes from the French word ragoût, or stew. It is said that the inventor of tagliatelle was inspired by the fine flaxen hair of Lucretia Borgia and that the inventor of tortellini, little stuffed rings of pasta, fell in love with his employer's wife when he saw her sleeping in the nude and promptly produced a new pasta in the shape of her navel.

Tortellini stuffed with turkey, sausage, ham, pork, egg and cheese are traditionally served on Christmas Day as a first course with a rich sauce of butter and cream and topped with grated cheese. Lasagne, baked in the oven with layers of meat and cream sauces, and cappelletti, "little hats," stuffed with ricotta, chicken, egg and spices, are other popular forms of pasta in Bologna.

Emilians are very fond of veal and serve it in their typically extravagant way, stuffed with cheese and ham and braised in wine, a habit that would horrify their plainer-living Tuscan neighbors.

In Emilia is the city of Parma, renowned throughout the world for its prosciutto or Parma ham, and for having given its name to Parmesan cheese. The original Parmesan is made in Reggio nell'Emilia and is known variously as parmigiano reggiano or formaggio di grana, "grained cheese" because of its finely-grained texture. It is probably the cheese most closely identified with Italian cuisine.

From Modena comes zampone, stuffed foreleg of pork, and from Piacenza *bomba di riso*, a pudding-shaped mold of rice cooked in white wine that contains vegetables and squabs cooked in red wine. In Ferrara the local delicacy is broiled eel and at Ravenna you can sample another Italian fish soup, *brodetto*.

The Ponte Vecchio in Florence, the city whose chefs and pastry cooks were responsible for educating the French in the culinary arts.

The Wines of Emilia-Romagna

The wines of this region are not as full and flavorsome as its cooking. Its most famous wine is Lambrusco, a dry sparkling red, beloved by the Bolognese and arousing strong reactions in visitors from outside the region, who are either captivated or repelled.

ALBANA
A well-balanced, yellow-gold wine grown around the town of Bertinoro. Light and fresh with a slight sweetness, but nevertheless delicious with fish.

CASTELFRANCO
A fragrant dry white wine from around Modena, made from a mixture of grapes grown in the same vineyard.

GUTTURNIO
A dryish, ruby-red wine, best drunk very young and served cool, made mainly from Barbera grapes.

LAMBRUSCO
Dry, red and sparkling, very pink and frothy when poured, but the bubbles subside to a tingle. The Bolognese say that its fresh, clean taste complements their rich cooking and that it aids the digestion.

SANGIOVESE
A fresh, ruby-red wine with a hint of garnet, widely grown throughout the region. Fruity when young, it mellows with age and is well prized by the locals.

SCANDIANO BIANCO
A popular, straw-yellow wine, this is not renowned for its quality outside the region. There are still dry and sparkling sweet varieties.

TREBBIANO
This grape is widely grown in the region, producing wines of different style and quality. The more common variety is drunk young, but there is also a sharp elegant wine that goes well with fish and a sweeter sparkling Trebbiano for dessert.

Liguria

This is the narrow strip of coast that stretches from San Remo to La Spezia and is bordered to the north by the Alps and Apennines. Its capital is the great port of Genoa and its culinary traditions, not surprisingly, reflect the seafaring nature of its inhabitants. For the fishermen who spent weeks at sea, food had to be prepared to keep. Lentils, garbanzo beans and dried beans, pies and savory biscuits were eaten at sea and when they returned home, the sailors satisfied their cravings for fresh green vegetables with tarts filled with artichokes, spinach, zucchini, Swiss chard and wild herbs – torta pasqualina. Genoa's favorite herb is basil, the main ingredient for pesto sauce. The word comes from "pestle." Basil, garlic, parmesan, olive oil and pine nuts – and sometimes lemon peel, beans and potatoes – are pounded together with a pestle in a mortar and served with gnocchi or pasta.

The land of Liguria is not good farming land, so every little bit of vegetation must be put to good use. One recipe calls for wild herbs, "the kind you find growing on the garden wall." The Ligurian frugality was responsible for the invention of ravioli – the word comes from robiole, or leftovers – little scraps stuffed into envelopes of pasta. *Cappon magro* is a true Genoese joke. Literally "thin capon," it is a dish that contains no meat at all. It is, for all that, a very majestic concoction and has been pronounced worthy of Homeric heroes. Layered boiled vegetables and pickled fish are built up to form a huge colorful dome which is then draped in a green sauce flavored with herbs.

Veneto

Veneto, with Trentio to the west and Friuli-Venezia Giulia to the east, is one of Italy's major wine producing areas and its famous exports include Soave, Valpolicella and Bardolino. Its gastronomic center is its capital, Venice, whose cuisine still reflects the legacy of the medieval spice trade. Here you can enjoy lightly curried fish and a delicate dish of peppered calf's liver and onions. The Venetians' taste is, on the whole, exotic. They like rice with jumbo shrimp, squid or shrimp in a garlic and tomato sauce, and even rice with grapes, cheese and garlic. Salt cod is cooked with cinnamon, turkey with pomegranate sauce and zucchini flowers are fried in butter.

Pasta is not much eaten in Veneto. Instead the locals favor polenta, which is not yellow as in most other parts of Italy, but white, made from the fine white corn grown in Friuli-Giulia. Another simple dish prized by the Venetians is *risi e bisi*, rice and peas. This falls somewhere between a soup and a risotto and is made at its best with the tender young peas available only in spring.

The merchants of Venice first introduced sugar into Europe and Venetians today still have a sweet tooth. In the middle of the morning the city is full of people sitting under awnings enjoying their *ombrina* – "little shade" – a glass of wine or a cup of coffee and sweet cornmeal cookies or the vanilla cake called pandoro.

A Genoese-style sponge cake which has its origins in Liguria.

Venice is a city of exotic culinary contrasts, a legacy from its position at the center of the spice trade in the Middle Ages. Here, some of the finest restaurants in Europe pay as much attention to the preparation of risi e bisi, a simple dish of rice and peas, as they do to scampi, oysters and caviare. Risi e bisi was, after all, the favorite dish of the doges.

The Wines of Liguria

Liguria is a small region and an even smaller wine producer, with most of the vineyards growing enough to supply only their owners' tables. Genoa is the center of the Italian wine trade, but it deals in the wines of the rest of Italy and drinks its own at home.

BARBAROSSA

So called because of the way the grape grows in "red beards." A festive pink wine, there is also a sweet variety.

CAMPOCHIESA BIANCO

A full-flavored dry white wine from the Pigato grape, Campochiesa improves with age. Traditionally it is laid down at the birth of a son to be drunk at his wedding.

CINQUETERRE

Drunk young, this is a delicate, clear, yellow-gold wine with a slightly bitter taste, made from the Vernaccia grape. It comes from five villages – hence its name – high up in rocky terrain. There is a sweet variety made from grapes part-dried in the sun. It has a high alcohol content (16%) and is much enjoyed with ice cream.

CORONATA

A dry white wine with a sharp fresh taste that goes very well with fish.

DOLCEACQUA

Made mainly from Rosesse grapes, this is a full, heavy aromatic wine that goes well with stronger flavored local dishes, such as pesto.

The Wines of Friuli-Venezia Giulia

The character of this region is more Slavic than Italian and the inhabitants are less patriotic than anywhere else in Italy. You are quite as likely to be served a Yugoslavian wine from Veneto as one grown locally.

GAMAY

A brilliant ruby-red wine from vines imported from France. Gamay grows well on the hills of the region and has a faint strawberry taste when young.

PICCOLIT

A golden-yellow dessert wine drunk chilled. It was much admired in European courts at the turn of the century and is best when it has aged a few years in the bottle. Piccolit grapes are part-dried in the sun after being picked to give the wine a more concentrated sweetness.

PINOT GRIGIO

Arguably the best white wine of the region, it has a slightly pink tinge and a faint tang of nutmeg. There are also smooth red and spumante versions.

SAUVIGNON

Another grape imported from France and grown widely throughout the region. An elegant, straw-yellow wine with a slightly bitter aftertaste.

TOCAI

A dry yellow-white wine quite unlike the Hungarian Tokay, which is a great dessert wine. Makes a very good accompaniment to fish dishes.

The Wines of Trentino-Alto Adige

Alto Adige, which its inhabitants call the South Tyrol, is German-speaking, and the wines have German names and are exported to Germany, Switzerland and Austria. The wines are finer and quite distinct from those produced in Trentino, which are less numerous.

BLAUBURGUNDER
A reliable, full red wine from the Pinot Noir grape grown around Bolzano, Caldaro and Terlano.

CALDARO
Luga di Caldaro is a full red wine with a slight almond flavor. Often called Kalterersee, the German name for the lake.

COLLINE BOLZANO
Red wines from the Schiavone grapes grown on the hills around Bolzano. Variable in quality.

GEWÜRZTRAMINER
In the South Tyrol is the village of Tramin, or Termeno, which the locals claim gave Gewürztraminer its name. But the white wine from this region is not as full or fragrant as its more famous namesake from Alsace.

RIESLING
A well-balanced wine, the Terlaner Riesling is one of the few whites of the area that are exported.

SANTA MAGDALENA
The finest red wine of this region – a brilliant ruby with a hint of orange, it is smooth with a slightly bitter aftertaste. Made from Schiava and Schiavone grapes, grown in the hills east of Bolzano.

The Wines of Veneto

One of the major wine-growing regions, Veneto produces Valpolicella, Bardolino and Soave, three of Italy's best known exports.

BARDOLINO
A bright, ruby-red wine with a fresh taste, made from a variety of grapes grown on the eastern shores of Lake Garda. Best drunk young and cool.

CABERNET
A full-bodied, vigorous red with a slight amber tint, best after it has spent at least three years in the bottle. It has woodland flavors of raspberry and honey with a hint of violet.

COLLI DI VALDOBBIADENE
A dry white with a hint of bitterness, and a sweet, slightly sparkling dessert wine, both bear this name.

MERLOT
A ruby-red wine with a fresh taste and a hint of almond. The Merlot grape is grown all over Italy; the Veneto Merlot is lighter than that from Trentino.

PROSECCO
A straw-yellow wine, aromatic and fresh. There is also a sparkling variety – Prosecco Spumante. Prosecco is grown all over the north of Italy.

RABOSO
A rather rough red wine common across the region, and best drunk young.

RECIOTO
A red wine so-called because it is made only from the "ears" *(orecchie)* of the bunches of grapes, which are riper than the rest. It is full and heavy and makes a good accompaniment to roast meat and mature cheese. A sweet sparkling variety can be drunk with dessert.

SOAVE
Smooth, dry and straw-yellow, this is one of the finest Italian whites. It is made mainly from Garganega grapes and is best drunk young and chilled as an accompaniment to the fish dishes of Venice.

VALPOLICELLA
Slightly fuller than Bardolino, this is the most popular red of the region. It can be aged in the bottle, but is perhaps best drunk cool and young.

Lombardy

Lombardy's national dish is risotto alla milanese, rice delicately flavored and colored with saffron. Another speciality is osso buco, braised veal shank on the bone, of which the marrow is considered to be the tastiest part. To the Milanese goes the credit of inventing another famous meat dish, the Wiener Schnitzel. The original Costoletta alla Milanese, the breaded veal chop, was taken back to Vienna in the 19th century by General Radetzky, and the Viennese promptly adopted them as their own.

Milan is Italy's financial capital and though the pace of life there is fast, cooking methods are traditionally slow and housewives spend long hours at the stove, braising, stewing, spit-roasting and gently simmering meat to succulent perfection. It is generally held in France that the Italians overcook their meat, and certainly they like it well done.

Though Lombardy is famous for its rice, it does not grow quite so much of it as Piedmont. It is primarily an area of wheat and dairy farming. Butter is the cooking medium and there are some excellent cheeses, among them gorgonzola. In Milan is the Via dei Ghiottoni, the street of gourmets (or gluttons), which is lined with food shops of every possible sort. One in particular, called Peck, is internationally renowned for its enormous selection of cheeses and its top-quality veal and cured meats. One of the more unusual of these is bresaola, beef salted and dried and sliced paper-thin to be eaten with olive oil, lemon juice and pepper.

Every visitor to Milan is sure to be offered a slice of panettone, a leavened cake made with eggs, raisins and candied peel that is the ideal breakfast accompaniment to a cup of coffee. Torrone is an almond-flavored dessert cake that has been a popular treat since the 13th century, and another favorite dessert is pears stuffed with Gorgonzola cheese.

Lombardy is a region of dairy farms and rice production. It is famous for gorgonzola and bel paese cheeses and for its tradition of long, slow cooking, which survives not only in small hilltop towns like this one but also in the region's capital, Milan.

The Wines of Lombardy

In the Valtelline, with the Alps to the north and the mountains of Bergamo to the south, the aristocratic Nebbiolo produces fine red wines as in Piedmont – Sassella, Grumello and Inferno. But they are quite elusive and inconsistent in quality and are often exported to Switzerland or appear under a brand name. The other main wine-producing areas are around Lake Garda and to the south of the Po in the Oltrepo Pavese.

CHIARETTO DEL GARDA

The red wines around Lake Garda are very light, and the rosés darker than the French ones. This is an intense pink wine made from a mixture of four types of grape. It has a sharp fresh taste and should be drunk young and cool. A good wine to choose for an outdoor lunch.

COLLINE DEL GARDA AND COLLINE MANTOVANE

Red, white and rosé wines from the area between Lake Garda and Mantua. The reds are very light and clear and all should be drunk young and cool.

FRANCIACORTA

A brilliant ruby-red wine with a fresh taste and a hint of raspberry.

FRECCIAROSSA

Frecciarossa is a village in the Oltrepo Pavese where the Odero family produce four fine wines bottled on their estate in the French style. Each has a brand name: the dry white is called "La Vigne Blanche," the medium dry white "Sillery," the rosé "Saint George" and the red, considered one of the finest Italian reds, is named "Le Grand Cru."

LACRIMA VITIS

A golden dessert wine made from Moscato grapes, partly dried in the sun after picking.

LUGANA

A fresh, dry white made from Trebbiano grapes and aged in the cask before bottling. It has a pale golden color and a slight saffron taste which goes very well with fish.

VALTELLINE REDS

Sassella, Grumello and Inferno are the great red wines of Lombardy, grown in terraces along the River Adda, which flows into Lake Como. They are made from 85 per cent of Nebbiolo grapes and benefit from aging in the bottle. Drink them with broiled and roast meat and game.

Piedmont

Piedmont is a mainly mountainous region and, as in other places with similar upland terrains, its diet is hearty, substantial and sustaining. However, its capital, Turin, also has a long tradition of culinary sophistication inherited from its great ruling House of Savoy, and this gives Piedmontese cooking a special edge of distinction that is lacking in other mountain areas. Side by side with robust peasant dishes of lasagne, polenta, gnocchi and boiled mixed meats are to be found delicacies such as trout baked on a bed of mushrooms, and the famous bagna cauda, which is a hot sauce of olive oil, butter, garlic and pounded anchovies. The latter is eaten as a dip for a variety of cold vegetables, among which is often the cardoon, or edible thistle.

Another delicious Piedmontese speciality is fonduta. This is a kind of fondue made with fat fontina cheese, cornstarch, milk and egg yolks, which is sometimes served poured over a slab of polenta and decorated with finely sliced truffles.

The frogs that breed prolifically in the Piedmontese rice fields are served up, appropriately enough, in risotto. Indeed, because Piedmont is the main rice-growing region of Italy, it would be suprising if rice did not feature large in Piedmontese cuisine. Another notable culinary feature of the area is that every meal is accompanied by grissini, the long crisp bread sticks that have become synonymous with Italian eating throughout the world. For dessert you might be offered a rich confection of chestnuts and cream called monte bianco, and after the meal a glass of grappa.

Macugnaga in Piedmont, Italy's prime rice-producing region. The hills here abound in goats and wild boar, and the woods yield up white truffles, which are prized even in France.

The Wines of Piedmont

Fine wines have been grown in Piedmont since Roman times. This is possible because the vineyards are gently sloping, the sun is not too fierce, and the vines are protected from the wind by the Alps. Most of the region's wine is full-bodied red, but it also produces the sparkling white Asti Spumante, favorite of many. Turin is the center of vermouth production, which mostly uses the cheaper wine of Apulia. The vermouth's aroma comes from the herbs which are to be found growing in the mountains nearby.

ASTI SPUMANTE

A sparkling, sweet white wine made from the Moscato grape, which is widely grown in Piedmont, Asti is made by the *cuvé close* method – fermented in closed vats and bottled under pressure. This is quicker and cheaper than the *méthode champagnoise*, which involves secondary fermentation in the bottle, and which is also used in this region to produce some sparkling dry whites, for example Gancia Royal Cuvée. Asti is a classic dessert wine that can also be enjoyed mid-morning or at parties.

BARBARESCO

A full-bodied, deep red wine made from the Nebbiolo grape, it matures early, taking on a slight amber tint. It comes from the hilly country near Alba.

BARBERA

Piedmont's commonest wine, this is a red that can vary greatly in quality. It can be slightly sparkling and sweet; it can be rather coarse when young but will acquire a mellow flavor with age. The best Barbera, which comes from around Asti, is granted a growers' association label of blue grapes on the city's red tower.

Fine wines have been grown in Piedmont since Roman times. This is possible because the vineyards are gently sloping, the sun is not too fierce, and the vines are protected from the wind by the Alps. Most of the region's wine is full-bodied red, but it also produces the sparkling white Asti Spumante, favourite of many. Turin is the centre of vermouth production, which mostly uses the cheaper wine of Apulia. The vermouth's aroma comes from the herbs which are to be found growing in the mountains nearby.

ASTI SPUMANTE

A sparkling, sweet white wine made from the Moscato grape, which is widely grown in Piedmont, Asti is made by the *cuvé close* method – fermented in closed vats and bottled under pressure. This is quicker and cheaper than the *méthode champagnoise*, which involves secondary fermentation in the bottle, and which is also used in this region to produce some sparkling dry whites, for example Gancia Royal Cuvée. Asti is a classic dessert wine that can also be enjoyed mid-morning or at parties.

BARBARESCO

A full-bodied, deep red wine made from the Nebbiolo grape, it matures early, taking on a slight amber tint. It comes from the hilly country near Alba.

BARBERA

Piedmont's commonest wine, this is a red that can vary greatly in quality. It can be slightly sparkling and sweet; it can be rather coarse when young but will acquire a mellow flavour with age. The best Barbera, which comes from around Asti, is granted a growers' association label of blue grapes on the city's red tower.

The Wines of Naples and the South

CAMPANIA
Wine has been cultivated here since Roman times, but Campania is not a region renowned for its fine wines. Much of what it produces today is for blending, and a great deal of it, of course, supplies the local tourist trade.

AGLIANICO
A robust red from the grape of the same name, which is grown all over southern Italy.

CAPRI
Red, white and rosé wines come from the island, but there are also mainland wines bottled under the same name. The white is a straw-yellow with a fresh taste and a hint of bitterness and highly thought of by the locals. All three are acceptable table wines made from a mixture of grapes.

COLLI SORRENTINI AND SORRENTO
Red, white and rosé wines, some of which appear as "Capri," or as "Sorriso di Sorrento," which particularly appeals to the more romantic tourist.

FALERNO
Both dry and sweet, white and red wines come from the plain north of Naples. The white is straw-yellow with a hint of amber and full flavor.

ISCHIA
Ischia Bianco is a delicate white, drunk young and chilled. It is made from a mixture of Biancolella and Fontana grapes. The reds from the island are not quite so individual, some being rather coarse.

LACRIMA CHRISTI
This is a very popular wine because of its memorable name (tears of Christ), but only the dry, German-style white lives up to its reputation. Other wines, including reds and rosés grown on the slopes of Vesuvius, are sold under this name and can be disappointing.

ABRUZZI-MOLISE
Craggy and mountainous, this region is not a great wine producer. What it does produce is either drunk locally or sent north for blending.

ABRUZZI BIANCO
A sharp, fresh white from the Trebbiano grape that makes a good accompaniment to fish.

ABRUZZI ROSSO
From the Montepulciano grape, which is grown widely throughout the region, this is very light red, sometimes with a slight tingle.

APULIA, BASILICATA, CALABRIA
In the hot south of Italy, wine production is the main source of income – in fact Apulia produces more wine than any other region of Italy. But because of the heavy soil and the fierce sun, and the fact that the vines are grown close to the ground so that extra heat is reflected up at them, the wine tends to be coarse and strong. The reds are used for blending and the whites as a base for the vermouth industry in Turin.

ALEATICO
A rich, sweet dessert wine from the grape of the same name. The must is taken off the skins of part-dried grapes and fermentation is halted by the addition of spirits. The result is quite strong (14°-17°).

CASTEL DEL MONTE
A fresh tingling white wine from the Bombino Bianco grape.

CASTELLANA
Red and rosé wines drunk very young and mainly used for blending.

LOCOROTONDO
Pips and skin are removed from a mixture of grapes to produce a characterless white wine used mainly as a base for vermouth.

Naples and the South

Naples is the gastronomic center of the south, just as Bologna is of the north, and it sets the tone of the cooking of Calabria, Basilicata, Apulia and Abruzzi-Molise, as well as its own region of Campania. Campania is the south's most fertile region and grows wheat, corn and millet as well as huge crops of all kinds of vegetables, especially tomatoes. All the ingredients are to hand for Naples' most celebrated and most exported dish, pizza. In Naples seafood is plentiful and a favorite spaghetti sauce is con vongole, with clams. Campania breeds the large white buffaloes whose milk is turned into mozzarella.

In the rest of the south, the land is mountainous, parched and poor. Olive oil rather than butter is the cooking medium – it costs less to keep an olive tree than a cow, and olive trees survive in poorer soil. Under the searing sun tempers run high, and the food is as fiery as those who eat it. Dried tubular pasta is served with angry sauces of garlic, hot peppers and burning chilies that take a little getting used to before their flavors can be truly appreciated.

The cooking of these poorer regions is largely based on pasta and vegetables, often cooked up together in a substantial soup. Fish soups of all kinds are made round the coast, but transport is difficult through the rocky terrain and fish is not often available inland. Instead, the locals keep chickens which scratch about in the streets, and make imaginative use of their hens' eggs, even combining them with sheep's tripe in one dish.

Amalfi (top) was the first Italian maritime republic and dates back to the 6th century. It is famed for its fish restaurants and one of its specialties is a dish of spaghetti with octopus, anchovies, shrimp and garlic.

Sicily and Sardinia

Sicily and Sardinia owe a lot of the distinctiveness of their cooking to the invaders from Greece, Phoenicia and Spain who have occupied the islands over the centuries. Both subsist mainly on a diet of pasta and bread, but Sicily produces early vegetables, olives and citrus fruit as well as wheat, while Sardinia is a pastoral island almost entirely devoted to rearing sheep and, to a lesser extent, goats.

From the Saracens, Sicily learned the art of making delicious sweets and pastries, among them cannoli, filled with cream cheese, chocolate and candied fruit, and cassata, a layered cake which includes the same ingredients plus liqueur, and is sometimes covered in chocolate. Baking is a national pastime in Sicily. There are large loaves like cartwheels and savory buns stuffed with pork, bacon and cheese.

Sardinians bake thin brittle circles of bread called *carta di musica*, music paper, and are fond of roasting whole sheep and goats, as well as wild boar, suckling pig and smaller game, on an outdoor spit. Instead of using herbs, they build their fires of aromatic woods, such as juniper or olive, to give the barbecued meat its distinctive flavor.

The island of Sardinia gave its name to the sardine, which swims in its waters along with lobsters and eels – and all these are cooked as simply as they were thousands of years ago.

The Wines of Sicily and Sardinia

Sardinia's inhabitants are unlike mainland Italians, being more somber and reserved. Their wines are just as individual, many of them being as strong as sherry without being fortified. The whites are pinkish and the reds so dark as to be called *vini neri* – black wines.

Most of the wines of Sicily are strong and rough as in southernmost Italy, and most are produced in large co-operatives and used for blending. The one major exception is Marsala, the distinctive dessert wine very popular throughout Italy as well as abroad.

The production of Marsala was set up around 1760 by a Liverpudlian, John Woodhouse, who visited the island and realized that the wine produced there resembled the base wines of port, sherry and Madeira.

The dry local white wine is fortified with wine brandy and sweetened with a local sweet wine made with part-dried grapes and unfermented grape juice, heated until it becomes syrupy.

Marsala is drunk as a dessert wine or an aperitif. It is also blended with egg yolks to make the rich, creamy dessert called Zabaglione.

Basic Equipment

Knives are of the utmost importance to the smooth functioning of an Italian kitchen. (1) large, sharp chef's knife; (2) vegetable paring knife; (3) decorative cutter with a corrugated edge; (4) fruit knife; (5) mezzaluna – a twin-handled, double-bladed chopper; (6) cleaver; (7) grapefruit knife.

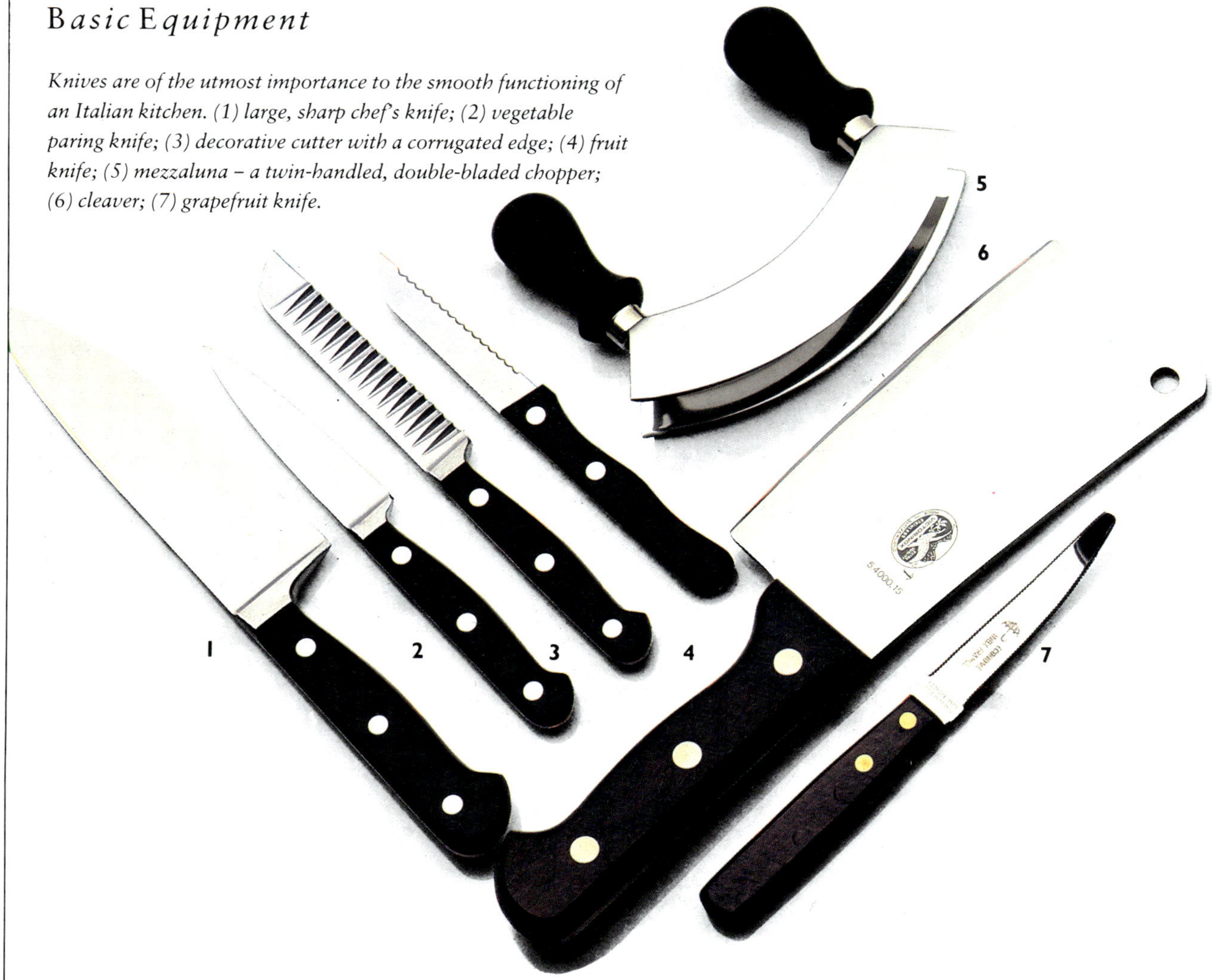

Many modern Italian kitchens now boast a hand-turned pasta rolling and cutting machine (left) *It ensures fine, even threads of tagliatelle and thin, smooth sheets of lasagne. A hand-held rotary cutter and a ravioli tray* (above) *are very useful for making meat, cheese, or vegetable-filled pastas.*

BASIC RECIPES

Pasta, gnocchi and pizza are probably the best-known components of Italian cuisine. Their popularity insures that they can be bought from most large supermarkets and some delicatessens – but nothing can quite compare with the taste of the genuine homemade article.

First column, top to bottom:
1 *wholewheat bucatini;* **2** *creste;* **3** *lumaconi;* **4** *green bigoli;* **5** *lasagne.*

Second column, top to bottom:
6 *maccheroncini (frilled macaroni);* **7** *sedanini;* **8** *vegetable macaroni;* **9** *long fusilli;* **10** *tagliatelli, fettucine.*

Third column, top to bottom:
11 *semolina spaghetti;* **12** *lumachine;* **13** *marille;* **14** *viti;* **15** *zite.*

Fourth column, top to bottom:
16 *large macaroni;* **17** *elbow macaroni;* **18** *penne;* **19** *green viti;* **20** *reginelle;* **21** *pappardelle.*

Fifth column, top to bottom:
22 *wholewheat spaghetti;* **23** *farfalle;* **24** *canelloni;* **25** *trenitte;* **26** *thin pappardelle or mafaldine.*

BASIC PASTA SHAPES

Pasta

A 1lb package of dried pasta will serve five people. Bring 7¾pints water to a boil in a large saucepan. Add a pinch of salt and about 1tsp oil. Add the pasta and increase the heat to get the water back to boiling point as quickly as possible. Cook it at a full rolling boil, stirring occasionally with a wooden spoon, for about 10 minutes. Remember that pasta continues to cook for a few moments when you take it off the heat so allow for this by stopping when the pasta is just *al dente.* When it is ready, add a cup or two of cold water to stop cooking and then drain. Meticulous draining is not necessary, as pasta should not dry out. (Italians say pasta is greedy for water.) The process is exactly the same for fresh pasta, but you will need about 8oz pasta per person, and the cooking time will be only about 4 minutes.

USING A PASTA MACHINE

The dough should be firmer than for hand-rolled pasta. Feed dough into the machine in small pieces, each rolled in flour, so it will not be so likely to stick to the blades.

Step-by-Step Homemade pasta

INGREDIENTS *serves 4*
$3\frac{1}{2}$ cups all purpose flour
4 medium eggs
vegetable oil

PREPARATION
Dust a board or working surface with flour. Mound the flour on to the board and make a well in the center. Break the eggs into it. Add 1tbsp cold water to the eggs and 1 or 2tsp oil. Beat the eggs with a fork and gradually work in the flour, using your hands when the dough becomes stiff. Knead for at least 10 minutes. The dough should be stiff – add extra flour if it is too soft. When little air bubbles start to appear, roll the dough into a ball, flatten then roll out with a rolling pin as far as possible, making sure that the thickness is uniform.

1 Make a well in the mound of flour, break in the eggs and beat with a fork.

2 Gradually work in the flour. When the dough stiffens, carry on using your hands.

3 Knead vigorously for at least 10 minutes.

4 When bubbles appear, roll the dough into a ball and then flatten it.

5 Roll out with a rolling pin. Starting from the center, roll out in all directions.

6 Turn the dough around, using a rolling pin.

7 Put it back down on the board and continue to roll out in the other direction.

HERBS

Basil

A wonderful aromatic herb which is decorative as well as useful. Basil is an excellent herb for flavoring tomato sauces to accompany pasta and an essential ingredient in the authentic Genoese pesto sauce.

Basil plants need the sun and a warm sheltered position. Pinching the tops of the plants will encourage the plant to bush and prevent flowers growing. If you move it to the kitchen window-sill in winter, you should manage to keep a small supply of fresh basil going for a couple of months.

Bay

Bay trees are ideal for balconies and patios. The tree should be kept in a sheltered postion in winter. When removing leaves for culinary use, take care not to spoil the shape. The occasional clipping of branches and constant picking of leaves will usually remove the need for heavy pruning. An essential ingredient in bouquet garni.

Bouquet Garni

This is a small bunch of fresh or dried herbs that are tied together with a piece of string. The string can be tied to the handle of a saucepan so that the whole bunch of herbs can be easily removed once it has imparted its flavor. Dried herbs are better placed in small cheesecloth bags.

There are now many different commercially prepared bouquet garni sachets for sale which are good substitutes for fresh herbs that are not available. Quality herbalists still pack the herbs in cheesecloth bags but the major commercial brands of bouquets garnis rather resemble teabags.

To make fresh bouquet garni, take and tie together one bay leaf, a good spring of thyme and two stalks of parsley, using a long thin string or thick thread.

Coriander (cilantro)

This distinctive plant with dark green glossy leaves is one of the hardier southern European herbs. It is used extensively in oriental cookery and is good for flavoring vegetable dishes as well as making a pretty garnish. Coriander can be grown in pots or tubs.

Dill

This is another pretty culinary herb that can be grown in tubs or pots. Fresh dill goes particularly well with many fish dishes and sauces. The long feathery fronds also make a pretty garnish.

Drying Herbs

Dry herbs in the dark and in a warm atmosphere such as a low oven or airing cupboard at approximately 100°F. The air must circulate freely around the drying herbs.

Freezing Herbs

The general rule for freezing is that only the leafy herbs such as parsley, chervil, coriander and sage retain their color and flavor really well.

Small packets of frozen herbs can easily be crumbled into sauces during cooking. The spiky leaves of thyme and rosemary are probably better dried.

Some fresh herbs can be frozen in ice-cube trays. Mint cubes, for example, are delicious in summer drinks.

Chives

This spiky herb belonging to the onion family is excellent for flavoring sauces and dressings. It grows well in pots and can usually be divided after a couple of years if grown in good soil. It freezes well for use in the winter.

Specially built raised beds of brick or stone add a decorative dimension to the patio or yard.

Marjoram/Origanum

The decorative wild marjoram is also easily grown in small containers and is suitable for flavoring sauces to accompany pasta. Its flavor is not quite as strong as that of the Mediterranean variety, origanum.

Mint

The many varieties of mint all have slightly different flavors. Experiment with two or three different mints until you find the ones you like best. The leaves are widely used in cooking. Mint leaves add taste and body to pasta salads and are also an attractive garnish. Two of the most popular varieties are apple mint and spearmint.

Parsley

Many varieties of parsley can be grown in large pots and tubs. Parsley can be used in quite large quantities and therefore it is cheaper to grow it from seed than to buy whole plants.

Rosemary

This is another plant discovered for the Western world by the Romans. It must be planted in a sheltered position to survive the winter in colder climates. Rosemary is a pretty, spiky bush and its aromatic leaves are a must for cooking, especially in lamb and vegetable dishes.

Sage

A distinctive plant with silvery leaves which has the advantage of being fairly hardy once it is established. The leaves are particularly popular in savory stuffings. This herb should be grown in a large pot and be left for a year before being robbed of too many leaves.

Thyme

This is yet another plant which comes from the Mediterranean region. There are several pretty varieties which can be grown in pots and they all provide flavorings for many of the classic sauces which accompany pasta. The little spiky leaves are evergreen and can be picked and used even in the winter.

Most Gardens, however small, have room for a herb garden. These designs confine each herb with bricks or paving stones, select plants that complement each other, either in flower color or leaf form and unless the area is extensive, avoid tall-growing herbs such as fennel.

Red pasta

INGREDIENTS *serves 4*
8oz carrots
1tsp tomato paste
$1\frac{3}{4}$ cups all purpose flour
3 eggs
pinch of salt

PREPARATION
The amount of flour used here will vary according to the moisture content of the carrots. Peel and steam the carrots and press through a fine strainer into a pan. Put the pan over heat and stir with a wooden spoon to dry out the purée. Stir in the tomato paste and let it cool. Proceed as with egg pasta (see page 33), adding the carrot mixture to the eggs in the flour well. Add more flour if necessary. This pasta, like the spinach variety, does not roll out as thinly as basic pasta dough. Treat it like plain egg pasta. Using three colors of pasta, you can prepare harlequin pasta.

Green pasta

INGREDIENTS *serves 4*
$\frac{1}{2}$ cup very well-drained cooked spinach
$1\frac{3}{4}$ cups all-purpose flour
3 eggs

PREPARATION
Press the spinach through a strainer or puree in a blender. Make the dough as usual, add the spinach and knead for 10 minutes. If the dough is too soft, add a little more flour. It is difficult to stretch out green pasta very thinly.

Tagliatelle

Tagliatelle is the simplest pasta shape to make – therefore it is probably the most commonly found. Make the pasta – white, red or green – as directed in the preceding pages. Roll out as thinly as possible, then, beginning at one end, roll the dough into a long, thin cylinder. Beginning at one end, cut the roll into slices. When the roll has been cut into slices gently ease the slices into separate strands of tagliatelle. Step-by-Step 1-2 *below.*

1 Using a knife with a wide blade, cut the roll into slices of the desired thickness.

2 Separate and spread out the shapes on the board.

Anolini

Cut out 2in circles. Fill with a nut-sized piece of meat filling and fold over the free pasta, making a little rim on the lower semicircle. Press the rim around the filling then shape the pasta around your left index finger.

Cappelletti

It is thought this pasta shape got its name from the alpine hats it resembles. Prepare the pasta as for tagliatelle (see above), and let it rest under a cloth. Using a little serrated cutter or a sharp knife, cut the pasta into squares with $1\text{-}1\frac{1}{2}$ in long sides. Place a pea-sized amount of filling in the middle of each square, then fold into a triangle. Then, keeping your left index finger under the filling, join the two points of the triangle, making sure that there is no hole (unlike agnolini). Stretch sideways a little, if necessary. Step 1 *right.*

1 To make cappelletti, use your hands and not the board.

Agnolini

Proceed as for tagliatelle (see page 34), making the dough a little firmer as it is to be rolled out more thinly. Cut squares 1in wide for serving in soup, otherwise 2in wide. Fill generously with stuffing and fold the pasta over. Put your index finger against the side of the pasta envelope and curve the pasta, joining the two ends. There should be a little hole in the center of the agnolino. Step-by-step 1-3 *below.*

1 Cut the pasta into strips 1in wide and place the strips on top of one another.

2 Using a sharp knife, cut the strips into squares.

3 Put your index finger against the side where the pasta was folded and turn two ends round your finger.

Cappelletti Toscani

Prepare the dough with 3 eggs to $3\frac{1}{2}$ cups flour and cut out circles. Put the meat filling in the center of each circle. Fold in half to make a semicircle. Holding the shape in your hands, press the edges around the filling, then join the two points of the half-moon shape. Do not turn the pasta up around the filling but leave it as it is, as though it were the brim of a little hat. There should be a small hole in the center. Step-by-step *right.*

1 Cut out circles on rolled out dough, place the meat filling on top, and fold in half.

2 Close the edges around the filling and press the seal flat. Join the corners of the half-circles together.

Tortellini and Tortelloni

Prepare the pasta as before and roll out. Cover the pasta with a cloth to avoid drying out, except in the area where you will be working. There are two basic tortellini shapes: square – like ravioli – and curved triangles with the edges joined. When these are large and served as a first course in sauce instead of in a broth, they are often called tortelloni. Both plain and green tortellini/tortelloni are popular. *Below* is a simple version of tortelloni verde al gratin. Step-by-step *right*.

Ravioli

These are common to all parts of Italy. They can be made with plain or egg pasta and are much like tortellini (see below). Make them square or round.

To make ravioli in the traditional fashion, roll pasta into a sheet, dot with filling, and then top with a second sheet.

1 Place a nut-sized piece of filling — either meat or ricotta and spinach — toward one corner of a square of pasta.

2 Fold the top over to form a triangle and join the points together to make a curved shape.

3 Place the tortelloni in a shallow dish and cover with a quantity of homemade tomato sauce.

4 Cover with a thick layer of mozzarella cheese. Cook for 45 minutes or until bubbling, then serve.

Tortelloni verde al gratin.

Potato dumplings (gnocchi)

INGREDIENTS *serves 4*

First Recipe

1¼lb russet potatoes
1 tsp salt
1 tbsp grappa, if desired
1 egg
1 cup all purpose flour

Second Recipe

1lb russet potatoes
1 tsp salt
2 eggs
1¼ cups all-purpose flour

PREPARATION

These gnocchi can be served with butter and parmesan, sage butter or a tomato sauce, meat sauce or pesto.

Peel the potatoes and boil them in salted water over low heat. Use even-sized potatoes, so that they cook evenly. When just tender, drain, and while still hot mash and put on to a board. Make a well in the middle of the mashed potatoes and put in the salt, grappa if using, and egg (or eggs). Then pour on the flour and mix well to give a firm dough that does not stick to your hands. The amount of flour will vary depending on how moist the potatoes are.

Knead the dough for some minutes. Cut off a piece of dough and roll into a cylinder on the floured board. Cut off 1in slices, roll into balls and flour well. Take a grater (or fork) and decorate the dumplings with holes or ridges, pressing in with your finger on one side to give a shell shape.

Bring a large pan of salted water to a boil and gently put in all the gnocchi at once. When they come to surface and float, remove with a slotted spoon, keeping the water boiling, and put in a casserole dish. Pour over the hot sauce of your choice, sprinkle with Parmesan, add a second layer of gnocchi etc. Put a cover on the dish and place over a saucepan of boiling water to let the gnocchi absorb the flavor of the sauce. Step-by-step *right*.

Both semolina and potato gnocchi are favorites of northern Italy. They are particularly popular as a dish for meatless holy days and Fridays.

1 Mash the potatoes, mix in the other ingredients and blend well.

2 Cut the dough into pieces, rolling out each one by hand.

3 Cut each piece into 1in slices, flour and mark with fork prongs on one side.

4 They can also be pressed against the reverse side of a grater.

Italian cooking tends to be uncomplicated in style, allowing fresh natural flavors to shine through. The displays of vegetables in prime condition in all Italian markets testify to their importance in Italian cuisine.

Semolina dumplings (gnocchi)

INGREDIENTS *serves 4*
3½ cups milk
salt
¾ cup fine semolina
½ cup butter
6 tsp Parmesan cheese
2 egg yolks
pepper
pinch of ground nutmeg
breadcrumbs

PREPARATION
These are sometimes thought to be a Roman speciality, but in fact they are eaten all over Italy.

Heat the milk with a pinch of salt, and when it boils gradually add the semolina, stirring the whole time with a wooden spoon to avoid lumps. Continue to cook, stirring, for 20 minutes. Remove from the heat and add 2 tbsp butter in small pieces. Then gradually stir in 2 tbsp Parmesan cheese, the egg yolks, one at a time, a pinch of pepper and nutmeg.

Oil one or two large dishes or a clean marble kitchen slab and pour the mixture on. Spread out to ½in thickness using a cold wet spatula and allow to cool.

Preheat the oven to 350°F. Melt the remaining butter; use some of the butter to grease a casserole. Cut out squares or circles of semolina dough and place in the greased dish. Drizzle with butter and sprinkle with Parmesan, add a second layer of gnocchi, and so on. Sprinkle the breadcrumbs over the gnocchi and bake for about 20 minutes or until golden brown. Step-by-step, *right*.

1 Pour the cooked semolina into a wide dish or on to a marble slab which has been lightly oiled.

2 With a metal spatula, spread to about 1cm/½in thickness.

3 With a biscuit (cookie) cutter or glass, cut the dough into discs.

4 Lift up the gnocchi and lay in a buttered dish.

Right: Neopolitan pizza; for recipe, see page 153

Polenta

Polenta can be made either from finely-ground cornmeal, coarser cornmeal or from buckwheat flour. The best pan for polenta is a copper one with a convex bottom to make stirring easier. Polenta should be cooked in the proportion of $1\frac{1}{2}$ cups cornmeal to $6\frac{1}{4}$ cups salted water, and this should not come more than halfway up the saucepan. The quantities vary according to how it is to be served. If a sauce is to be served with it, for four people you will need $3\frac{1}{2}$ cups cornmeal and $11\frac{1}{4}$ cups water. For coarse meal, boil the water, then add the meal gradually in handfuls, stirring to avoid lumps. The cooking time will vary from 40 minutes to about an hour. Stir the mixture constantly, scraping the sides and bottom. When the polenta comes away easily from sides of the pan at the end of the cooking time, loosen it from the pan with a slotted spoon moistened in cold water, and turn out. Serve the polenta very hot. If you use finer cornmeal, add a fifth of it to the cold water before putting it on to boil, then cover the pan and bring to a boil. Boil for 10 minutes, then gradually add the rest and proceed as before.

Pizza dough

INGREDIENTS *serves 4*

1oz fresh yeast (1 cake compressed yeast) or 1 package active dry yeast
1 cup all-purpose flour
pinch of salt

PREPARATION

Pizza is not commonly made at home in Italy, but is eaten in a pizzeria. It is a speciality of Naples.

Crumble the yeast into a cup and dissolve in about $\frac{1}{4}$ cup lukewarm water 95°. For dry yeast, use warm water (110°F. Mix in about $\frac{1}{4}$ cup of flour, cover the cup with a cloth and leave in a warm place to rise. Put the remaining flour into a bowl, add a pinch of salt and put the yeast mixture in a well in the middle. Work in the yeast mixture gradually, adding just enough water to make the dough smooth and pliable. Knead for 10 minutes, then roll the dough into a ball, put in a floured bowl, cover and let rise in a warm place until the dough has doubled in bulk. Once risen, the dough is ready to be made into pizzas.

For homemade pizza you can buy ready-made bread dough, to which you just need to add 1tbsp oil, knead and roll out. This is a much quicker method than making pizza dough from scratch. Step-by-step *right.*

1 Measure the fresh or dried yeast and the flour carefully. Sieve the flour into a large bowl.

2 Make a well in the center of the flour and pour in the yeast mixture and a little lukewarm water.

3 Using a palette knife or spatula, mix until you have a firm, plastic dough. If extra water is required, work in carefully to avoid the dough becoming sticky.

4 Turn the dough out on to a floured board and knead vigorously for 10 minutes.

5 Place the dough in a lightly floured bowl. Cover with plastic wrap. Put in a warm place and allow to double in bulk.

6 Turn the risen dough on to a floured board. Knead and punch down until all air pockets are eliminated. The dough should be smooth, firm and elastic.

ANTIPASTI

Antipasti are savory morsels designed to whet the appetite. Serve an attractive arrangement of eggs, olives, pickled vegetables, artichoke hearts, asparagus, and anchovies, or paper-thin slices of prosciutto with melon or figs, or choose from any of the following recipes.

Roast Vegetables in Oil

INGREDIENTS *serves 2/4*

1 yellow, red or green pepper per 2 people
1 eggplant per 4 people
1 zucchini each
⅔ cup olive oil per 4 people
salt and freshly ground black pepper to taste

PREPARATION

Preheat the oven to 370°F. Halve the peppers and de-seed them. Cut off the coarse stem of the eggplant and trim the zucchini.

Lay the peppers and eggplant directly on to the oven shelves. Do not baste them. Cook for 10 minutes, then add the zucchini.

Remove all the vegetables after 15 minutes' cooking, when they will be soft.

Now slice the peppers and eggplants as you will. Simply cut the zucchini in half lengthways.

While everything is still hot, brush with the oil and season to taste. Pour over what remains of the oil and serve hot, cold or at room temperature.

Chef's tip

The vegetables steam in their own juices and thus intensify their own natural goodness. *Basta!*

Page 44: Roast vegetables in oil

Baked Stuffed Tomatoes

INGREDIENTS *serves 4*

8 large ripe tomatoes
1 onion, finely chopped
vegetable oil
8 anchovy fillets, rinsed well, pounded to a paste
1 bunch parsley, chopped
3 tbsp capers
2 tbsp breadcrumbs
¼ cup sliced ripe olives
salt and pepper
ground nutmeg (optional)

PREPARATION

Preheat the oven to 350°F. Cut a lid from the top of each tomato and reserve. Scoop out some of the flesh, seed, chop and set aside. Turn the tomatoes over and drain.

Fry the onion in a little oil; add the chopped tomatoes, anchovies, parsley, capers, breadcrumbs and olives. Season with salt, pepper and a little nutmeg, if desired, and mix well. Divide between the tomatoes; stuff the tomatoes. Top each with reserved top slice.

Put the tomatoes in a baking dish, drizzle oil over them and bake for 30 minutes.

Above: Baked stuffed tomatoes

Parmesan

Parmesan is the best-known of all Italian cheeses. It accompanies pasta and rice and is ideal for cooking because it does not turn stringy as it melts. It is also delicious at the end of a meal with fruit. If you can avoid it, never buy pre-grated Parmesan sold in cartons – it has no taste. Parmesan bought by the chunk should be pale yellow and finely honeycombed – the generic name for this cheese in Italy is grana, referring to its fine grain. The best grana is four years old and correspondingly expensive. Store large pieces of Parmesan wrapped in two or three sheets of foil in the bottom of the fridge.

Above Asparagus with Parmesan and fried eggs.

Below:
A selection of Italian cheeses;
1 *Parmesan (grana);* **2** *Pecorino;*
3 *Fontina;* **4** *Gorgonzola.*

Asparagus with Parmesan and Fried Eggs

INGREDIENTS *serves 4*

2lb fresh asparagus
salt to taste
1/3 cup butter
1/2 cup freshly-grated Parmesan cheese
2 tbsp olive oil
4 eggs

PREPARATION

Preheat the oven to 375°F. Trim the coarse whitish ends from the asparagus spears.

Boil the asparagus in salted water for about 10 minutes. (If you can keep the heads above the surface of the water, so much the better. Steamed, they have a better chance of remaining intact.)

Grease the bottom of a flat, oven-proof dish with one-third of the butter. It should be large enough to accommodate the asparagus in two layers only.

When the asparagus has cooked, arrange it in the dish.

Sprinkle the Parmesan over the asparagus and dot it with the remaining butter then bake until the cheese and butter form a light brown crust – about 10 minutes.

In the meantime, fry the eggs carefully. You must not break the yolks.

To serve, divide the asparagus into four portions on heated plates. Slide a fried egg over each portion. The crusty, cheesy asparagus is dipped in the egg yolks and eaten by hand with precious little finesse but much enjoyment.

Broiled Mussels

INGREDIENTS *serves 4/6*

2lb fresh mussels
2 cups fresh breadcrumbs
½ cup freshly-grated Parmesan cheese
4tbsp finely chopped parsley
4 large cloves garlic, finely chopped
salt and freshly ground black pepper to taste
⅔ cup olive oil

PREPARATION

Preheat the oven to 400°F. Thoroughly scrub the mussels, removing all beards and barnacles.

Place a pan of water large enough to hold them all on a low heat, add the mussels and cover. Cook for about 5 minutes.

In the meantime, combine the breadcrumbs, Parmesan, parsley, garlic, salt and pepper in a bowl.

Take the mussels off the heat, drain, and set aside the liquor.

Remove the top shell from each mussel, leaving the flesh ensconced in the lower shell. Discard any mussels which have failed to open. Lay the half-shell mussels on a baking tray and sprinkle the breadcrumb mixture into each shell.

Combine the oil and the reserved mussel liquor and pour a little on to each mussel. Return stuffed mussels to a hot broiler, or the preheated oven, and bake for 3-4 minutes.

Oven-Crisped Bread with Tomato and Fresh Basil

INGREDIENTS *serves 6*

6 slices thickly-cut white bread, preferably Italian
1lb fresh tomatoes
½ cup fresh basil
⅔ cup olive oil
salt and freshly ground black pepper to taste

PREPARATION

In a low oven, toast the bread until each slice is completely dry and crisp.

Roughly dice the tomatoes (there is no need to peel them), and finely chop the basil.

Add the basil, olive oil and seasoning to the tomatoes.

Spoon on top of the bread slices and serve immediately. (The bread should still be slightly warm).

Below: Broiled Mussels

Above: Sardines with pepper and tomato sauce.

Sardines with Pepper and Tomato Sauce

INGREDIENTS *serves 4*

12 sardines in oil
1 green or red pepper, roasted, skinned, cut into strips
whites of 3 hardboiled eggs, chopped
$1\frac{1}{4}$ cups peeled, seeded, chopped tomatoes
2tbsp butter
few fresh sage leaves, chopped
1 clove garlic, crushed
salt and pepper

PREPARATION

Bone the sardines carefully and reassemble them on a serving dish. Decorate with the pepper and egg whites. Press the tomatoes through a strainer and cream with the butter, sage and garlic. Season with salt and pepper and spoon over the sardines.

Mozzarella in Carozza

INGREDIENTS *serves 4*

10 slices square white bread, crusts trimmed
thinly sliced mozzarella cheese
all-purpose flour
2 eggs
1-2tbsp whipping cream or milk
salt
vegetable oil or butter

PREPARATION

Cover half the bread slices with cheese. Press the remaining bread on top. Pour cold water into a bowl and put a little flour into a second bowl. Dip each sandwich first in the flour, then water, holding the edges firmly, and arrange on the bottom of a large dish.

Break the eggs into a cup, beat with the cream or milk and a pinch of salt, and pour over the sandwiches. Turn the sandwiches over to coat completely with egg mixture. Let stand for 10 minutes.

Heat some oil or butter in a skillet and brown the sandwiches on both sides. Serve very hot.

Sardines

Sardines are known by many different names in Italy. The Italians say the sardine has 24 virtues and loses one every hour – therefore it should be eaten very fresh. To prepare fresh sardines, slit open the stomach and pull out entrails and the backbone. Cut off the head, if preferred. Fresh sardines are delicious broiled over an open fire with a little rosemary, black pepper and lemon juice or dipped in flour, egg and breadcrumbs and fried.

Raw Beef Fillet Perfumed with Garlic, Anchovy and Lemon

INGREDIENTS *serves 4*

1¼ cups olive oil
4 large cloves garlic
4 anchovy fillets
2 whole chili peppers
1lb fillet steak
salt and freshly ground black pepper to taste
juice of 2 lemons

PREPARATION

Heat the oil over a low heat until it is hot, but not hot enough to fry.

Add the garlic, anchovy fillets and the chili peppers and let them stew in the oil for 20 minutes. (On no account should there be any sizzle. You are not frying these ingredients but letting their flavors soak into the oil.)

While the marinade is cooking, slice the beef as finely as you can. There is no such thing as too fine. Lay the slices out on a flat dish, lightly salt them, add pepper to taste and pour over the lemon juice.

Remove the oil from the heat after 20 minutes. Allow it to cool then pour it over the beef.

Chill the dish for 12 hours. Before serving, remove the garlic and any intact pieces of anchovy. The chilies can be left.

Left: Raw beef fillet perfumed with garlic, anchovy and lemon

Chef's aside

This dish requires a very sharp knife. It is best eaten with unbuttered very fresh Italian bread, with which you can also mop up the juices.

Parmesan Cheese Fritters

INGREDIENTS *serves 4*

4oz fresh Parmesan cheese in one piece
3½ cups all-purpose flour
pinch of baking powder
salt
¾ cup butter or solid vegetable shortening, slightly softened, diced
vegetable oil or vegetable shortening for frying parsley

PREPARATION

Cut the Parmesan into thin slivers, or grate coarsely. Pour the flour, baking powder and 1 tbsp salt on to a board. Make a well in the center and add ½ cup + 2 tbsp butter or shortening. Rub well into the flour and add enough lukewarm water to form into a dough. Knead for 10 minutes and then roll out to a thin rectangular sheet.

Arrange little heaps of cheese at intervals in a row 2in from edge of pastry. Dot piles of cheese with remaining 2 tbsp butter or shortening. Fold pastry over cheese and press down well with your fingers.

With a pastry cutter or a knife, cut off filled strip and cut around each mound of cheese, making sure the edges are well sealed into squares or oblongs.

Fry filled pastries in plenty of hot oil or shortening. Remove when golden brown and puffed up and drain on paper towels. Arrange on a serving dish, garnish with parsley and serve very hot.

SOUPS

Soup would not be served in Italy at the same meal as pasta, because it often contains pasta itself. An Italian soup may be a delicate consommé garnished with dumplings or eggs, or it may be a nourishing broth thickened with rice and vegetables. Offer Parmesan cheese with anything other than a fish soup.

Minestrone

INGREDIENTS *serves 6/8*

¼ cup butter
¼ cup olive oil
3 large onions
2 cloves garlic
8oz carrots
2 sticks celery
8oz potatoes
8oz cooked white kidney beans
4oz French beans
4oz zucchini
3 beef bouillon cubes *or* 6¼ cups Pastine in Brodo (see page 56)
½ cup chopped fresh or canned Italian tomatoes
⅔ cup piece of Parmesan cheese rind
salt and freshly ground black pepper to taste

PREPARATION

Melt the butter together with the oil over a medium heat. Finely chop the onions, garlic, potatoes, carrots and celery and add them, one vegetable at a time, to the oil and butter in a large pot. Cook each for 2-3 minutes, without browning.

Stir in the white and French beans. Chop the zucchini into larger pieces and add them to the mixture.

Crumble in the bouillon cubes and stir in 6¼ cups water. Stir in the chopped tomatoes and add the whole cheese rind.

Cook the whole mixture together until you have a substantially thick soup – a consistency you must decide for yourself. Once your desire is satisfied in this matter, add water to maintain the consistency, if necessary, until the soup is thoroughly cooked – about 20 minutes. Season before serving and remember to remove the piece of cheese rind.

Page 52: Minestrone

Chef's aside

This is one version of *minestrone*. There are about as many as there are combinations of vegetables. Sometimes they contain pasta, sometimes rice and sometimes the mixture is thick with lentils. There are just two serious rules: use a lot of vegetables and don't forget the cheese rind.

Country Garbanzo Soup

INGREDIENTS *serves 4*

1lb dried garbanzo beans
¼ cup chopped pancetta
1 green onion, chopped
1 clove garlic, sliced
1tbsp chopped parsley
pinch of dried leaf marjoram
2 tbsp vegetable oil
⅔ cup peeled, chopped tomatoes
¾ cup chopped lean pork
salt and pepper
4 slices toast
½ cup grated Parmesan cheese

PREPARATION

Soak the garbanzo beans in lukewarm water for 12 hours. Put the pancetta, green onion, garlic, parsley and marjoram into a pan. Stir in oil, drained garbanzo beans and tomatoes; add enough water to cover. Bring to a boil.

Add pork, reduce heat to medium, cover and simmer for 2 hours. Season with salt and a pinch of pepper and mix. Lay slices of toast in bottom of four soup bowls and pour the soup on. Pass Parmesan separately.

Garbanzo beans

Garbanzo beans are often served in Italy with pasta (in a dish called tuoni e lampo – thunder and lighting) or in soups. The dried ones should be soaked for 12 hours and simmered for between two and six hours until tender. As this is a lengthy process, it may be wiser to buy the canned variety.

Garnishes for soups

Soup is often a substantial dish in Italy and the garnishes are correspondingly hearty. Choose from pasta shapes, bread croûtons – fried or baked in the oven, and sometimes stuffed as well – or dumplings made of potato or semolina and mixed with spinach, chicken, ham or fish and Béchamel Sauce (page 122).

Bean Soup with Parsley, Garlic and Chili

INGREDIENTS *serves 4*
- ¾lb dried white kidney beans
- 4 cloves garlic
- 4 tbsp olive oil
- 4 tbsp tomato paste
- 2 tbsp finely chopped fresh parsley
- 1oz fresh chilies
- salt and pepper to taste

PREPARATION

Soak the kidney beans in double their volume of water overnight. Leave the pot near a low heat source, a radiator or pilot light, if you can.

A minimum of 1½ hours before you wish to serve the soup, drain the beans, cover them with more water and set them to boil over a low heat. Cook them for between 40 and 60 minutes, until they are tender. If you are using them immediately, let them stand in their cooking water. Otherwise, drain and store covered in the fridge.

Peel and crush the garlic and soften it in the olive oil over a low heat. As it begins to color, drain away as much of the oil as you can and set it aside.

Add the cooked beans, the tomato paste, the parsley and no more than ½pt of water. Bring the mixture to a boil then lower the heat to simmer.

As the soup is cooking, slice and seed the fresh chilies and stew them very gently in the garlic-flavored olive oil until they are very soft. Pour the chili oil into a small serving bowl.

Take half the quantity of the bean soup and liquidize it. When the consistency is completely smooth, combine the two parts of the soup.

Check the seasoning. The soup is now ready to serve.

Above: Bean soup with parsley, garlic and chilli

Chef's tip

The chili oil is used as a highly-spiced condiment alongside the soup. The soup has a very thick, rich consistency and a soothing flavor. The chili oil provides a remarkable contrast.

Minestrone Livorno *style*

INGREDIENTS *serves 4*

1lb unshelled fresh lima beans
2 tbsp chopped parsley
1 slice prosciutto
1 clove garlic
olive oil
½ small head leafy cabbage, shredded
⅔ cup trimmed, washed, shredded spinach
1 onion, chopped
1¼lb potatoes, peeled, cut into julienne strips
½ cup julienne-cut carrot
1 stick celery, cut into julienne strips
1 zucchini, cut into julienne strips
1 bouillon cube
1½ cups peeled, seeded, chopped ripe tomatoes
4oz salt pork, blanched, cut into strips
salt
⅔ cup rice
5tbsp grated Parmesan cheese

PREPARATION

In winter this can be prepared with dried soaked beans and canned tomatoes. Shell the beans and put them into cold water.

Finely chop parsley, together with prosciutto and garlic. Put this in a skillet with 3 tbsp oil. Cook for a few minutes, then add cabbage and spinach, stir and continue to cook over medium heat.

Add onion, potatoes, carrot, celery and zucchini. Pour in 5 cups water, add bouillon cube, tomatoes and salt pork. When the water comes to a boil, add drained beans, cover and simmer gently for 2 hours. Season to taste with salt, add rice, stir and cook, uncovered, until rice is done. The soup should be thick. Remove from heat and stir in 2 tbsp Parmesan. Serve remaining Parmesan separately.

Egg *Noodle* Soup

INGREDIENTS *serves 4*

3 eggs
3 tbsp fine semolina
1tbsp chopped parsley
¼ cup grated Parmesan cheese
7½ cups beef stock
salt
ground nutmeg

PREPARATION

In a bowl, beat eggs with semolina, parsley and 2 tbsp Parmesan. Pour in a cup of cold stock, season with salt and nutmeg and whisk. Bring remaining stock to a boil, pour in semolina mixture and stir for 3-4 minutes over medium heat until fine shreds of egg form in the soup. Serve at once, sprinkled with remaining Parmesan.

Chef's tip

It is only the truly assiduous who teach themselves broth and stock making. For that reason, you will find frequent references to bouillon cubes as you proceed. Of course, a better substitute in all cases is homemade stock and the recipe for Pastine in Brodo shows how the Italians do it. You will note that it is very light and delicate. Please keep it that way – in the fridge if you wish. Use it as often as you can in place of cubes.

Pastine in Brodo

INGREDIENTS *serves 4-6*

1 medium onion
1 large carrot
2 sticks celery
1 small fennel bulb
½ medium fresh green pepper
1 medium potato
1 ripe fresh tomato (about ¼lb)
2lb assorted meat scraps and bones
8oz dried pasta stars
salt and pepper to taste

PREPARATION

Put all the ingredients except the pasta and the salt into 2¾pt cold water.

Bring the liquid very slowly to just under the boil and hold it there. (Boiling makes stock cloudy, so don't.) Cook for 3 hours. Skim the broth constantly, or, when it is cooked, allow to cool and then lift off the solidified fats. (This will considerably lengthen the preparation process.)

When the broth is cooked and skimmed, add the pasta. Since you have carefully removed all the fats, you may now boil it. Do so for about 10 minutes, or until the pasta shells are just soft. Salt and serve.

Rice and Peas

INGREDIENTS *serves 4*
¼ cup butter
1tbsp olive oil
1 small onion
2lb fresh peas, shelled (*see* Chef's Tips)
1 bouillon cube *or* 3 cups Pastine in Brodo (see page 56)
8oz Arborio (risotto) rice
2 tbsp finely chopped fresh parsley
⅓ cup freshly grated Parmesan
salt and pepper to taste

Above: Rice and peas

PREPARATION
Melt the butter and olive oil together over a low heat.

Finely chop the onion and soften it in the oil/butter mixture. Add the peas and cook them for a further 2 minutes.

Crumble in the bouillon cube and add 3 cups water. Bring the mixture to a boil.

As the water (or broth) boils, add the parsley and the rice. Cook for about 15 minutes until the rice has softened but remains firm – al dente.

Whisk in the grated Parmesan, season with the salt and finish with a generous twist or three of black pepper.

Chef's tips

You could use frozen peas but then why not make fish fingers? The real point of this extraordinarily simple dish is the spiky flavor of fresh peas – so cook it only when the season is right. The texture, incidentally, is midway between soup and risotto, and requires a spoon.

Lentil Soup

INGREDIENTS *serves 4/6*
2 tbsp olive oil
1 medium onion
1 stick celery
2 slices bacon or pancetta
8oz fresh or canned tomatoes
8oz brown or green lentils
1 beef bouillon cube or 6¼ cups Pastine in Brodo (see page 56)
3 tbsp freshly grated Parmesan cheese
2 tbsp butter
salt and freshly ground black pepper to taste

PREPARATION
In a good sized pan, heat the olive oil over a medium flame.

Very finely slice the onion and soften it in the oil. Finely slice the celery and add it to the onions when they are soft. Cook on for a further 2 minutes or so.

As the celery is cooking, dice the bacon. Add it to the mixture.

Roughly chop the tomatoes and add them to the soup, together with the lentils.

Crumble in the bouillon cube and add 6¼ cups water. Bring to a boil on a high flame and then reduce to a simmer. You must cook the soup until the lentils are tender, up to 45 minutes. Test by tasting the soup occasionally. When the lentils are soft, season with the salt.

Off the heat, whisk in the butter and Parmesan. Pour the mixture into a suitable tureen, and generously coat the top with fresh black pepper.

Below: Lentil soup

Rice and Turnip Soup

INGREDIENTS *serves 4*

2 tbsp parsley sprigs
2 strips bacon or pancetta
butter
2 medium turnips, peeled, thinly sliced
5½ cups beef stock
¾ cup rice
6 tbsp grated Parmesan cheese

PREPARATION

Finely chop parsley together with bacon. Fry for a few minutes in a little butter. Then add turnips and cook for a few minutes. Add stock, bring to a boil and simmer for 7 minutes. Add rice, stir and cook, uncovered, until just al dente.

A minute before removing from heat, stir in 2 tbsp Parmesan, then serve, passing remaining cheese separately. If turnips are very young and tender you can add them when you put in the rice.

Egg Pasta and Pea Soup

INGREDIENTS *serves 4*

½ carrot, chopped
½ onion, chopped
½ stick celery, chopped
1 tbsp chopped parsley
2 tbsp butter
1 tbsp tomato paste
salt and pepper
¾ cup shelled young, fresh petits pois
¾ cup small egg pasta shapes
½ cup grated Parmesan cheese

PREPARATION

Gently fry carrot, onion, celery and parsley in a pan with butter until golden brown. Add tomato paste diluted with 2 tbsp water, season with salt and pepper and cook for 10 minutes. Pour in 6 cups water, bring to a boil and add peas. Cook for 25 minutes, add pasta and cook for a further 15 minutes. Serve at once, passing cheese separately.

Above: Rice and turnip soup

Pancetta

Each region of Italy has its special kind of salami. Sometimes the meat is fine ground, giving a smooth texture and a pale pink color, or it may be coarse ground so that the sausage has large chunks of dark red and white meat, often dotted with black peppercorns.

Pancetta is the same cut of pork as bacon, but cured in salt and spices instead of being smoked. It is rolled into a sausage shape and sold sliced.

Mussel and Potato Soup

INGREDIENTS *serves 4*
$1\frac{1}{2}$lbs mussels
vegetable oil
freshly ground black pepper
2 strips bacon
$\frac{1}{2}$ small onion
1 clove garlic
$1\frac{1}{2}$ cups peeled, sliced potatoes
salt
$\frac{3}{4}$ cup rice

PREPARATION
Pull off and discard the beards from the mussels, rinse the mussels well under cold running water. Cook in a large pan over low heat with a little oil and a pinch of freshly ground pepper until they open. Drain, reserving liquid, and discard any mussels that remain closed. Remove the mussels from their shells.

Chop the bacon, onion and garlic finely together and put into a pan with 1 tbsp oil. Pour in $5\frac{1}{4}$ cups water, add potatoes, season with salt and bring to a boil. Simmer for 10 minutes, then add the rice and cook briskly.

Just before the soup is cooked, strain the reserved mussel cooking liquid and add to the soup with the mussels. Heat through for a couple of minutes and serve.

Poached Egg in Broth

INGREDiENTS *serves 6*
6 cups light broth (see Pastine in Brodo on page 56)
6 slices good Italian bread
6 eggs
3 tbsp freshly grated Parmesan
salt and freshly ground black pepper to taste

PREPARATION
Bring the broth to a boil. As the broth is heating, toast the slices of bread to a light brown and set each in the bottom of an ovenproof soup dish.

Distribute the broth evenly between the dishes. Now carefully break an egg into each dish, over the slice of bread. Do not split the egg yolk.

Put the bowls into a pre-heated oven and bake for 10 minutes or until the eggs are just set. Sprinkle each with the fresh Parmesan, season and serve.

Above: Poached egg in broth

Left: Mussel and potato soup

Tuscan Fish Soup

INGREDIENTS *serves 4*

2lb assorted fresh whole fish, large and small
1¼lb assorted seafood, including squid, shrimp, etc.
1¾ cups mussels or clams
2 tbsp parsley sprigs
3 cloves garlic
1 red chili pepper
olive oil
1 large onion, thinly sliced
1 stick celery, thinly sliced
1 carrot, thinly sliced
salt and pepper
½ cup dry white wine
3 medium ripe tomatoes, peeled, seeded, sliced
4 large *or* 8 small slices firm white bread

PREPARATION

This delicious fish soup can easily be a main course in itself. Any seafood can be used: mullet, eel, shrimp, crayfish etc, provided it is very fresh.

Clean fish, keeping heads to one side, leaving small fish whole and cutting big ones into equal-size chunks. Wash and drain well. Clean and prepare squid; shell and devein shrimps. Then clean mussels or clams, washing very well. Soaking for a couple of hours helps to get rid of any sand.

Wash and trim the parsley and chop it together with 2 cloves garlic and the chili pepper. Put this mixture with ¼ cup oil into a large saucepan over medium heat. Add onion, celery and carrot, season with salt and pepper and fry gently, stirring well. Then add seafood and fish and cook gently, gradually stirring in wine. When wine has evaporated, add mussels or clams. When they have opened, remove and reserve.

Add tomatoes and continue cooking until squid is done, adding a little water, if necessary. Meanwhile, poach fish heads separately in water for about 15-20 minutes. Discard bones; push flesh through a strainer or purée in a blender. Stir purée into soup. If mixture is very thick, add a little boiling water. Season to taste.

Preheat oven to 375°F. Rub bread with remaining clove garlic and put on a baking sheet in oven. When bread has hardened, lay slices in a large tureen or in individual soup bowls. When soup is done, remove bones if you wish, correct seasoning and pour over bread. Serve immediately, accompanied by the same wine you have used for cooking.

Above: Tuscan fish soup

Crazy-cut Pasta Romagnola Style

INGREDIENTS *serves 4*

1¼ cups all-purpose flour
3 eggs, beaten
salt
pinch of ground nutmeg
6 cups chicken or beef stock

PREPARATION

Heap the flour on a work surface, make a well in the middle and add eggs and a pinch of salt and nutmeg. Form into a dough and knead mixture until it is smooth. Form dough into a rectangular loaf shape and leave to dry out a little. Cut it into thick slices and let dry a little longer. Chop coarsely and dry out completely. Pour the stock into a pan and bring to a boil. Add pasta and cook for 2-3 minutes, then serve in soup bowls.

Minestrone with Pesto

INGREDIENTS *serves 4*

8oz fresh spinach
6oz fresh green beans
2 potatoes, peeled, sliced
½ head green cabbage, chopped
1 leek, sliced
½ onion, sliced
2 tbsp vegetable oil
salt and pepper
1 tbsp pesto sauce (see page 132)
¾ cup rice

PREPARATION

Wash, trim and chop the spinach. Put in a pan with the beans, potatoes, cabbage, leek and onion. Stir in oil to coat. Season with salt and pepper and add 6 cups water. Bring to a boil and cook over medium heat for 1 hour. Stir in the pesto, pour in the rice and cook for 15 minutes longer. Serve at once.

Potato and Onion Soup

INGREDIENTS *serves 4/6*

4 tbsp butter
2 tbsp olive oil
1½lb onions
2lb potatoes
1½ beef bouillon cubes *or* 3¾ cups Pastine in Brodo (see page 56)
3 tbsp freshly grated Parmesan cheese
salt and freshly ground black pepper to taste

PREPARATION

Melt the oil and butter together over a high heat. Finely chop the onions and cook them in the oil and butter until they turn light brown. Remove the pan from the heat.

Peel and dice the potatoes and boil them with the bouillon cubes and 3¾ cups water until they are quite soft.

Now turn the potatoes and their water into the onion pan – which still contains the onions – and cook on together for a further 10 minutes. As the mixture cooks, press the potatoes into the sides of the pan to loosen any caramelized onion residue.

Stir the cheese into the soup, season and serve forthwith.

Above: Potato and onion soup

Red Lettuce and Rice Soup with Fresh Sage

INGREDIENTS *serves 4*

3 tbsp olive oil
1 small onion
2 cloves garlic
1 large head radicchio
1 chicken bouillon cube or 3¾ cups Pastine in Brodo (see page 56)
8 tbsp Arborio (risotto) rice
1 heaping tbsp freshly grated Parmesan cheese
5 tbsp *fresh* finely chopped sage — nothing else will do
salt and freshly ground black pepper to taste

PREPARATION

Heat the olive oil over a medium flame. Finely slice the onion and sauté it until it softens. It must not color. Add the garlic, unchopped.

As the garlic and onions stew together, finely shred the radicchio. Add it to the pan and cook it until it softens completely – about 3-4 minutes.

Crumble in the bouillon cube and add 3¾ cups water. Add the rice and cook everything together until the rice is cooked but still firm – al dente.

Whisk in the Parmesan and the finely chopped sage. Cook on for another minute or so. Season and serve.

Below: Red lettuce and rice soup with fresh sage

Radicchio

A speciality of Treviso, radicchio is shaped like a small round lettuce, but is rose-colored with cream veins. Radicchio from Castelfranco has darker streaks against a lighter ground. Purists say the two should never be mixed.

Ancora

PASTA, GNOCCHI AND POLENTA

Pasta is traditionally made at home in central and northern Italy, and produced in factories and sold in packages in the south. Now, with more women out at work, both fresh and dried pasta are readily available in the shops, but there is still nothing quite like making it yourself.

Spaghetti Morgan

INGREDIENTS *serves 6*
1lb dried spaghetti
salt to taste
1¼ cups olive oil
3 cloves garlic
1 medium onion
2lb fresh plum or canned tomatoes
1tsp sugar
1 large eggplant
2 tbsp finely chopped fresh basil (one-third quantity, if using dried)

PREPARATION
Set the water to boil and salt it. As the water is heating, heat ¼ cup olive oil in a deep skillet. Crush the garlic, slice the onions and soften them together in the oil.

Roughly chop the tomatoes and add them to the onion mixture when it is softened. Add the sugar and turn the heat down to simmer.

In a deepish pan, heat the remaining olive oil until just below smoking temperature. As the oil heats up, cut the eggplant into small ¼in dice.

Fry the eggplant dice, a batch at a time, until the flesh is cooked to a wrinkled mid-brown. Set aside the cooked pieces on kitchen paper.

Cook the pasta until al dente; drain.

Stir the eggplant into the tomato sauce and throw in the finely chopped basil. Check the seasoning and serve with the pasta immediately.

Page 64: Spaghetti Morgan

Vegetable Lasagne

INGREDIENTS *serves 4*
¼ cup oil
1 eggplant, sliced
1 red pepper, seeded
1 zucchini, sliced
salt and freshly ground pepper
2 cups mushrooms, sliced
2 cups Tomato Sauce II (page 126)
2½ cups Béchamel Sauce (page 122)
9 sheets cooked lasagne (page 75)
Parmesan cheese

PREPARATION
Preheat the oven to 350°F. Heat the oil and fry the vegetables over a low heat, filling the pan and turning in the oil for about 3 minutes each batch. You will need to allow 15 minutes for preparing and frying the vegetables.

Start with the tomato sauce and one third of the vegetables. Top with Béchamel Sauce and lasagne. Season and start layering as in Lasagne al Forno (see page 75) ending with Béchamel and cheese.

When all the ingredients are used, bake until golden brown in the oven (about 25 minutes).

Chef's aside

The pungent flavor of the crisped eggplant, and the fresh and practically uncooked strands of basil makes this sauce truly special. It comes originally from Sicily, where it was probably named after the pirate.

Veal and Chicken Pasta *Stuffing*

INGREDIENTS *for 1lb pasta dough*
1 small onion, peeled
1 clove garlic
2 tbsp oil
⅓ cup cooked chicken
½ cup ground veal
1tbsp fresh breadcrumbs
1tbsp Parmesan cheese
salt and freshly ground pepper
½ tsp brandy (optional)
1tsp chopped parsley
a few spikes of fresh rosemary
a few leaves or 1tsp dried thyme
½ egg, beaten

PREPARATION
Dice the onion finely and crush the garlic. Heat the oil and cook the onion and garlic for 4 minutes over a low heat until transparent. Remove with a slotted spoon into a bowl.

Place the ground veal in the oil and fry over a medium heat for 5 minutes, separating with a fork as it cooks; add the chicken for the last 2 minutes. Spoon into the bowl.

Add all the remaining ingredients and mix well with the egg. Allow to cool and use as required for stuffing pasta.

Above: Rolled broiled eggplant stuffed with spaghetti

Rolled Broiled Eggplant Stuffed with Spaghetti

INGREDIENTS *serves 6*

2 medium eggplants
1lb spaghetti
salt
4tbsp olive oil
3 cloves garlic
1 medium onion
2lb fresh or canned plum tomatoes
1tsp sugar
2 tbsp finely chopped basil (one-third the quantity, if using dried)
3 tbsp freshly grated Parmesan cheese

PREPARATION

Preheat the oven to 350°F. Slice the eggplants lengthways into ½in strips. Roast them as for Roast Vegetables in Oil (see page 46).

Prepare the pasta in the normal manner.

Cook half the oil together with the garlic, onion, sugar and tomatoes as for Spaghetti Morgan (see page 66). Add the basil, however, as soon as the sauce is cooked in about 20 minutes. When the pasta is cooked, drain it and allow to cool a little.

Top each slice of eggplant with a thin layer of pasta. Spread tomato sauce on top of that. Roll the eggplant slice up into a long bundle. Secure it with a toothpick.

Arrange the bundles on a baking tray and brush them with the remaining oil. Sprinkle with the Parmesan and return to the oven and bake until the cheese forms a light crust on top.

When serving, spoon over what remains of the sauce.

Above: Ravioli with sage and pumpkin

Spicy Vermicelli

INGREDIENTS *serves 4*
1lb vermicelli
8 flat anchovy fillets
1 clove garlic, chopped
vegetable oil
2 red chili peppers, chopped
1tbsp chopped parsley

PREPARATION

Boil the vermicelli in plenty of salted water until *al dente*, drain and put on a serving dish. Meanwhile, prepare the sauce. Thoroughly rinse the anchovies and pound in a mortar. Fry the garlic in oil until soft. Add the chili peppers, anchovies and parsley. Pour sauce on the vermicelli and serve.

Fettucini Roma

INGREDIENTS *serves 4*
1lb fettucini
4 tbsp butter
½ tsp ground nutmeg
⅝ cup cream
salt and freshly ground pepper
⅔ cup Parmesan cheese

PREPARATION

Bring a well filled saucepan of salted water to a boil, add a few drops of oil and salt. Feed in the fettucini and cook until *al dente* – fresh pasta will only take about 2 minutes. Drain in a colander.

Melt the butter in the saucepan, add ground nutmeg. Pour in half the cream and stir until shiny and bubbles start to appear.

Add the fettucini and stir around in the pan. Pour in the remaining cream and cheese alternately, forking the pasta as it is mixed. Serve immediately.

Ravioli with Sage and Pumpkin

INGREDIENTS *serves 4*

For the pasta
3½ cups all-purpose flour
salt
5 eggs
1tsp vegetable oil

For the filling
4¼lb pumpkin, seeded
½ cup grated Parmesan cheese
4 crushed amaretti biscuits
coarse-grained mustard *or* Italian fruity mustard, if available
salt and pepper
pinch of ground nutmeg

For the sauce
½ cup melted, browned butter
few fresh sage leaves, chopped
⅓ cup grated Parmesan cheese

PREPARATION

Preheat the oven to 400°F. For the pasta, follow instructions on page 33, mixing a pinch of salt with the flour. For the filling, bake the pumpkin until tender and scrape the flesh into a bowl. Mash the pumpkin well. Stir in the Parmesan, amaretti cookies, and the mustard. Season with salt, pepper and a pinch of nutmeg and mix well. To prepare ravioli, make according to instruction on page 77, placing the filling at 2-2½in intervals. Boil the ravioli in plenty of salted water until *al dente*. Drain and arrange in layers in a baking dish, topping each layer with melted, browned butter, sage and Parmesan. Finish with a sprinkling of Parmesan. Bake in the oven until golden brown.

Right: Hay and straw with cream and raw ham

Macaroni Cheese with Bacon and Tomato

INGREDIENTS *serves 4*

1 cup short cut macaroni
salt and freshly ground pepper
$\frac{1}{2}$ tsp oil
1tbsp butter
$2\frac{1}{2}$ cups Mornay Sauce (see page 123)
$\frac{1}{2}$ cup grated cheese
1tbsp fresh breadcrumbs
4 slices of back bacon
2 tomatoes, sliced

PREPARATION

Preheat the oven to 400°F. Cook the macaroni for 7 minutes in boiling salted water to which a few drops of oil have been added. Drain well.

Preheat the oven to 400°F. Butter an ovenproof dish and prepare the sauce. Mix the macaroni with the sauce and pour into the dish. Sprinkle with grated cheese mixed with fresh breadcrumbs.

Arrange the bacon slices on top of the macaroni alternately with tomato slices. Cook in the oven for 15-20 minutes until bacon is cooked.

Prosciutto

Parma ham, prosciutto, is made from the boned hind legs of the pig. It is first salted and then dried – the air in the hills around Parma being ideal to bring it to maturity. It is sliced paper thin. The tender, sweet, light red meat is popularly served as an appetizer with fresh figs or melon.

Hay and Straw with Cream and Raw Ham

INGREDIENTS *serves 4*

8oz plain noodles
8oz spinach noodles
salt
$1\frac{1}{4}$ cups heavy cream
1 tbsp finely chopped fresh sage
1 tbsp finely chopped fresh parsley
$\frac{2}{3}$ cup dry white wine
4oz Parma ham
2 tbsp butter

PREPARATION

Cook the pastas in the usual way. Bring the heavy cream to a boil, and then add the sage, parsley and dry white wine. Keep boiling to reduce the volume of liquid by one third (i.e. to the original volume of the cream).

When this is done, dice the ham and add it to the cream. Remove from the heat.

When the pasta is cooked, drain it and whisk in the butter. Toss it in the mixture and serve very hot.

Spaghetti with Clams

INGREDIENTS *serves 4*

1 onion, peeled
2 cloves garlic, crushed
4 tbsp olive oil
6 beef tomatoes, peeled and diced *or*
1½ cups canned tomatoes
4 tbsp white wine
salt and freshly ground pepper
1 small can clams
2 tbsp freshly chopped parsley
¾lb spaghetti
1tbsp butter
pinch of nutmeg

PREPARATION

Dice the onion finely, peel and crush the garlic. Heat the oil in a saucepan or large skillet and cook over a low heat until the onion is transparent.

Add the tomatoes, white wine and seasoning. Simmer for 10 minutes. Add the drained clams and heat gently for a further 6 minutes.

Meanwhile cook the spaghetti in plenty of boiling salted water for about 12 minutes. Drain and toss in a little melted butter, add a shake of pepper and nutmeg.

Add the parsley to the sauce and stir well. Combine with the clam sauce and serve at once on heated plates.

Note: If you are using fresh clams scrub the shells and wash well in several batches of cold water to remove sand and grit. Place them in a skillet with 2 tbsp of white wine and cook over a high heat until the shells open. Strain and use the juice in the sauce. Remove the fish from the shells and heat through the sauce as above.

Ricotta and Parmesan Stuffing

INGREDIENTS *for 1lb pasta dough*

1⅓ cups ricotta cheese
⅓ cup Parmesan cheese
2 tbsp chopped parsley
1 tbsp fresh breadcrumbs
¼ tsp nutmeg
½ tsp marjoram
salt and freshly ground pepper
1 egg, beaten

PREPARATION

Mix all the ingredients in a bowl and add the egg slowly so that the mixture does not become too wet.

Use as required to stuff pasta shapes.

Variation: Ricotta and Spinach Stuffing
Use 1 cup ricotta cheese. Drain ⅓-½ cup fresh, frozen or canned spinach. Chop spinach and mix with all other ingredients.

Spaghetti with clams

12 % VOL

Spaghetti with Bacon *and* Eggs

INGREDIENTS *serves 4/5*

$\frac{1}{2}$ cup diced pancetta
$\frac{1}{4}$ cup butter
4 eggs
$\frac{1}{4}$ cup whipping cream
pepper
1lb spaghetti
$\frac{1}{3}$ cup grated Parmesan cheese

PREPARATION

Fry the pancetta in butter, remove with a slotted spoon and keep hot. Beat the eggs in a large bowl with cream and a pinch of pepper. Cook the spaghetti *al dente* in plenty of boiling salted water, drain, pour into a bowl with the eggs and mix well. Sprinkle with the pancetta and Parmesan and serve at once.

Pasta

Taste in pasta divides Italy roughly into two. In the north of Italy and as far south as Rome the pasta is mainly of the ribbon variety – flat, fresh and home-made with egg. Around Naples and further south it is tubular, eggless, mass produced and dried.

Pasta for soups includes conchigliette (little shells), anellini (little hoops), nocchette (little bows) and semini (little seeds).

Pasta to be boiled includes fettucine (ribbons), fusilli (spirals), spaghetti, ziti (fat spaghetti) conchiglie (shells), penne (nibs), cappelletti (hats), farfalle (bows), macaroni and ruote (wheels).

Pasta to be stuffed includes lumache (snails), cannelloni, ravioli, and tortellini.

M*acaroni with* S*hrimp*

INGREDIENTS *serves 4*

1tsp dried leaf thyme
1 bay leaf
2 tbsp chopped parsley
salt
$1\frac{1}{2}$ cups uncooked shrimp unshelled
1lb macaroni
2 cloves garlic, crushed
vegetable oil
1 red chili pepper, chopped
$1\frac{3}{4}$ cups peeled, chopped tomatoes

PREPARATION

Put the thyme, bay leaf, 1 tbsp parsley and a pinch of salt into a pan of water, bring to a boil and add the shrimp. Cook for 3 minutes, then drain. Shell, devein and coarsely chop the shrimp. Cook the macaroni in plenty of boiling salted water until *al dente*. Fry garlic in oil, add chili pepper and tomatoes, season with salt and cook for 10 minutes. Add the shrimp. Drain the pasta, mix in the sauce and sprinkle on the remaining parsley.

P*asta* T*rio*

INGREDIENTS *serves 4*

$1\frac{1}{3}$ cups stuffed ravioli or tortellini
$1\frac{1}{4}$ cups Béchamel Sauce (see page 122)
8oz tagliatelli
1 cup Tomato Sauce II (see page 126)
8oz wholemeal twistetti
$1\frac{1}{4}$ cups Bolognese Sauce (see page 130)

To garnish
$\frac{2}{3}$ cup Parmesan cheese

PREPARATION

For this dish you can serve any of your favorite pastas and sauces.

Cook the pasta, starting with that which has the longest cooking time, drain the water into a bowl and return the pasta to the saucepan and keep it warm.

Keep the three sauces warm.

Serve on individual dishes on a large plate accompanied by a bowl of Parmesan cheese and green salad.

accompanied by a bowl of parmesan cheese and green salad.

Spaghetti Quick-Baked in Foil with Cream, Shrimp and Brandy

INGREDIENTS *serves 6*

1 lb spaghetti
salt to taste
1¼ cups heavy cream
2 tbsp finely chopped fresh parsley
¼ cup brandy or cognac
1⅔ cup peeled uncooked shrimp (cooked can be substituted, if necessary)
freshly grated black pepper

PREPARATION

Preheat the oven to 375°F. Set the pasta to cook in the usual manner on the top of the stove.

As the pasta is cooking, bring the cream to boiling point in a saucepan. Add the parsley to the cream, together with the cognac. Remove the cream from the heat. Let it stand so that the flavors infuse.

Now finely chop the shrimp. If they are uncooked, add them to the cream and return it to the heat until it reboils. There is no need to bring cooked shrimp to a boil.

When you are ready to drain the pasta, spread out on a baking tray a sheet of foil large enough to fold over and completely envelop both pasta and sauce. Place the drained pasta in the middle of the foil and pour the sauce on top. Lift the edges of the foil upwards around the pasta and fold them together, completely sealing the contents.

Bake the parcel in the hot oven for about 5 minutes, then transfer the foil intact to a serving dish. Unseal at the table, sprinkle with black pepper and serve.

Above: Spaghetti quick-baked in foil with cream, shrimp and brandy

Lasagne al Forno

INGREDIENTS *serves 6*
1lb dried lasagne
salt
$\frac{1}{4}$ cup olive oil
2 cloves garlic
1 medium onion
2lb fresh or canned plum tomatoes
1tsp sugar
2 tbsp fresh basil (one-third the quantity, if using dried)
$2\frac{1}{2}$ cups Béchamel Sauce (see page 122)

PREPARATION
Preheat the oven to 425°F. Cook the strips of lasagne until just soft in a large pot of boiling water and little olive oil. Remove from the water, drain them, and lay them out, not overlapping, on a lightly-greased work surface.

Using a little over half the oil, make a tomato sauce as for Spaghetti Morgan (see page 66).

Grease the bottom of a 12in baking dish with the remaining oil. Cover it with a layer of the cooked pasta.

Spoon a layer of the tomato sauce on to the pasta, followed by a layer of the Béchamel. Proceed thus until the dish is full: pasta, sauce, Béchamel, pasta, sauce and so on. (Ensure you retain sufficient Béchamel for a generous final coating.)

Bake in the very hot oven for 15-20 minutes, or until the top has browned well and begun to crisp at the edges.

Left: Lasagne al Forno

Chef's tip

Baking pasta is a commonplace and you can do it with all kinds and with many sauces. Simply make sure the pasta is well sauced and covered or it will dry out.

Chicken and Mushroom Lasagne

INGREDIENTS *serves 4/6*
1 onion, peeled and diced
2 tbsp butter
2 cups mushrooms, washed and sliced
2 cups cooked chicken, diced
2 tbsp fresh breadcrumbs
$2\frac{1}{2}$ cups Béchamel Sauce (see page 122)
3 tbsp grated Parmesan cheese
9 sheets lasagne
salt and freshly ground white pepper

PREPARATION
Preheat the oven to 350°F. Cook the onion in the butter over a low heat for about 3 minutes. Add the mushrooms and cook for a further 2 minutes. Add the chicken to the mushroom and onions, season well and mix with chopped parsley. Make up the Béchamel Sauce, season well.

Place about 4 tbsp sauce in the bottom of an ovenproof dish. Cover with one third of the chicken mixture. Place sheets of "non-cook" lasagne on top to cover. If using fresh it can be cooked in boiling water for 3 minutes.

Place a further 4 tbsp sauce on top of the lasagne and a further third of the chicken mixture. Continue with third layer of lasagne, and top with the remaining Béchamel Sauce.

Mix the fresh crumbs with the cheese and sprinkle on top. Bake in the oven for 25 minutes until golden brown.

Tagliatelle with Basil, Pine Nuts *and* Parmesan Cheese

INGREDIENTS *serves 6*

1 lb tagliatelle

salt

¼lb fresh basil leaves (dried just will not do)

⅔ cup olive oil

3 tbsp pine nuts

2 cloves garlic

⅓ cup freshly grated Parmesan cheese

3 tbsp freshly grated pecorino cheese (optional)

PREPARATION

Prepare the pasta in the usual way. Put all the ingredients except the cheeses in the blender; process to a fine paste. If you have no blender, you must use a mortar and pestle. In this case, add the olive oil after you have blended all the other ingredients.

Whisk in the cheeses by hand and only then check the salt: the cheeses may well be salty enough. (You may blend the cheeses along with the other ingredients, if you wish, but you will find the texture rather too smooth if you do.)

When the pasta is ready, drain it and toss it in the pesto.

Above: Tagliatelle with basil, pine nuts and Parmesan

Bucatini with Bacon *and* Tomatoes

INGREDIENTS *serves 4*
$^1/_2$ cup chopped pancetta
2 tbps solid vegetable shortening
1 small onion, finely chopped
2 cups peeled, seeded,
  chopped firm-ripe tomatoes
salt and white pepper
1 lb bucatini (or other pasta shapes)
$^1/_4$ cup grated pecorino cheese

PREPARATION
Put on plenty of salted water to boil for the pasta. Put the pancetta in a saucepan with shortening and onion and fry until browned. Add the tomatoes, season lightly with salt and white pepper and cook briskly for about 10 minutes. Meanwhile, cook pasta until *al dente*, drain, transfer to bowl, add cheese and sauce, stir and serve piping hot.

Spaghetti with Chicken Livers

INGREDIENTS *serves 4*
1 lb chicken livers, diced
1 red pepper, seeded
1 clove garlic, crushed
4 tbsp butter
salt and freshly ground pepper
4 tomatoes, skinned and chopped
2 basil leaves, chopped
1 lb spaghetti
oil
freshly chopped parsley (optional)

PREPARATION
Prepare the chicken livers by cutting into small pieces. Cut and dice the pepper finely. Blanch it for 2 minutes in water that has just boiled and drain. Crush the garlic.

Melt the butter in a skillet and simmer the garlic and pepper for 5 minutes. Add the chicken livers and stir round, mixing with the pepper. Cook for 5-6 minutes on a low heat. Add the tomatoes, basil and seasoning.

While the sauce is simmering cook the spaghetti in boiling salted water with a few drops of oil. Drain and mix well with the chicken liver sauce. Each portion can be garnished finally with some freshly chopped parsley.

Making Ravioli

Mark the rolled dough (which has not been allowed to rest after rolling) with a pastry wheel into 1in squares. Place the stuffing in the squares and top with the other strip of pasta. Cut around the squares with the wheel and place on a flat tray.

To make the ravioli in a shaped tray, roll the pasta in to strips a little larger than the tray, line the tray with pasta and place the filling in each of the square sections. Cover the whole with another strip and roll over the top with a rolling pin. The ravioli shapes will seal and the tray can be turned over to release the ravioli.

Gratin of Ravoli *with* Cream

INGREDIENTS *serves 4*
For the pasta
$1^3/_4$ cups all-purpose flour
salt
5 eggs
1 tbsp oil

For the filling
2 tbsp chopped onion
3 tbsp butter
12oz finely diced sausage
2 tbsp breadcrumbs
salt and pepper
2 egg yolks
2 tbsp grated Parmesan cheese

For the sauce
$^1/_2$ cup butter
5 tbsp grated Parmesan cheese
about 1 cup half and half

PREPARATION
Preheat the oven to 400°F. For the pasta, follow the instructions on page 33, mixing a pinch of salt with the flour. For the filling, soften the onion in butter, add the sausage, breadcrumbs, salt and pepper and cook gently for 10 minutes. Transfer the sauce to a bowl and allow it to cool. Mix in the egg yolks and Parmesan. Assemble ravioli according to the instructions. Boil the ravioli in plenty of salted water for about 7 minutes or until they rise to the surface of the water and lose their pasty appearance. Drain and arrrange in a baking dish in layers; dot each layer with butter, sprinkle with Parmesan and drizzle with half-and-half. Bake until golden brown.

Gnocchi with Gorgonzola

INGREDIENTS *serves 4/6*
1lb potato gnocchi (see page 37)
salt
1 cup milk
4 tbsp butter
4oz Gorgonzola, crumbled into tiny pieces
2 tbsp freshly grated Parmesan cheese
¼ cup heavy cream

PREPARATION
Boil the gnocchi as you would pasta. But watch as they will cook more quickly – 3 to 4 minutes should be quite sufficient.

As the gnocchi are cooking, heat the milk in a pan large enough to hold all the ingredients, including the gnocchi. As soon as the milk is warm, reduce the heat to a low simmer. Add the butter, the crumbled Gorgonzola, and the Parmesan. Slowly beat everything into a creamy paste. Remove from the heat.

As soon as the pasta is cooked, drain it and add it to the sauce. Over a very low heat, stir in the cream. Serve instantly.

Broiled Polenta with Gorgonzola

INGREDIENTS *serves 6*
¾lb cooked and cooled polenta (see page 38)
½lb Gorgonzola cheese

PREPARATION
Cut the cold, set polenta into manageable blocks and carefully cut each block into 1in slices.

Heat the broiler to maximum and toast each slice on both sides, until the surface begins to brown and bubble.

Spread one side of each polenta slice with the Gorgonzola cheese. Return it to the broiler. Serve as soon as the Gorgonzola cheese has melted.

Fried Polenta with Mushrooms

INGREDIENTS *serves 6*
2 tbsp olive oil
2 tbsp butter
1½lb field or wood mushrooms or ceps (*funghi porcini*), roughly chopped
2 cloves garlic, roughly chopped
2 whole small chili peppers, roughly chopped
¼ cup red wine
1 medium tomato, roughly diced
1tbsp finely chopped fresh parsley
1tbsp finely chopped fresh sage
¾lb cooked and cooled polenta (see page 38)
salt and pepper to taste

PREPARATION
Melt one-third of the oil and the butter together over a medium flame. Add the mushrooms, garlic and chilies and fry together for 3-4 minutes over a high heat. Add the wine, tomatoes, parsley and sage to the mixture. Reduce the flame to a simmer.

As the mixture is cooking, slice the cold polenta as for broiled polenta (see Broiled Polenta).

In a large, open pan, heat the remaining oil over a high flame. Fry each slice on both sides until a thin crust forms. Keep the slices hot if you do the frying in more than one batch.

When all the polenta is fried, season the mushroom mixture and spoon it generously over each slice. Serve immediately.

Left: Gnocchi with gorgonzola

Spinach Gnocchi

INGREDIENTS *serves 4*
1 cup cooked spinach
1⅓ cups ricotta cheese
⅓ cup Parmesan cheese
salt and freshly ground pepper
1 tbsp butter
4 tbsp all-purpose flour
¼ tsp ground nutmeg

PREPARATION
Drain the cooked spinach well. Either chop finely or add gradually to a blender or food processor. The mixture must be creamed together with the cheese – this will take only a few seconds in the machine.

Mix the eggs in a bowl and season well and add the sifted flour and nutmeg. Add the spinach mixture and mix well. The food processor will mix the dough.

Leave in the refrigerator for at least half an hour, preferably longer, to chill.

Flour a pastry-board or work-top and knead the mixture for a few minutes with floured hands. Take small pieces and roll into 2in lengths.

Drop the gnocchi into a saucepan of boiling salted water and cook for about 10 minutes. Drain well and serve with a little melted butter and Parmesan cheese.

Gnocchi with Chicken Livers

INGREDIENTS *serves 4/6*
1lb potato gnocchi (see page 37)
salt
2 tbsp olive oil
2 cloves garlic
1 small onion, very finely chopped
1tbsp finely chopped fresh sage
⅔ cup red wine
8oz chicken livers
⅔ cup heavy cream

PREPARATION
Cook the gnocchi in the usual manner.

Heat the oil in a skillet, throw in the whole cloves of garlic and the onion. Soften in the oil until the onion begins to brown.

Add the sage and the red wine; reduce the volume of the wine by half over a high heat. Remove.

When all the gnocchi are ready, bring the red wine mixture back to a boil and toss in the livers, very finely chopped. Cook for a minute or so, then add the cream.

Bring the pan back to a boil, check the seasoning and, off the heat, gently stir in the gnocchi. Serve immediately.

Above: Gnocchi with chicken livers

PASTA FROM THE MICROWAVE

Pasta dishes are of long-established tradition, but this doesn't mean they can't be cooked in an up-to-date way. Microwave ovens are a boon in the modern kitchen and can produce pasta dishes that taste every bit as good as those produced by a conventional cooker – but in a fraction of the time.

Tagliatelle with Vegetables and Ham

INGREDIENTS *serves 4*

1tbsp olive oil
1 clove garlic, crushed
1 small onion, chopped
2 zucchini, chopped
1 small red pepper, diced
1¼ cups mushrooms, wiped and sliced
2oz ham, chopped
¾ cup canned tomatoes, drained and mashed
salt and freshly ground black pepper
14oz tagliatelle
chopped parsley
Parmesan cheese

PREPARATION

Put the oil in a bowl and cook on full power for 30 seconds. Add the garlic and onion and cook on full power for 2 minutes. Add the zucchini, red pepper and mushrooms, cover with vented plastic wrap and cook on full power for 3 minutes. Add the ham and tomatoes, cover and cook on full power for 2 minutes. Season to taste. Keep warm.

Put the tagliatelle in a deep pot, just cover with boiling water and add a pinch of salt and a few drops of oil. Cover and cook on full power for 6 minutes. Let the pot stand, covered, while you reheat the sauce if necessary.

Drain the pasta, pour on the sauce, sprinkle with parsley and serve with plenty of Parmesan cheese.

Left: Tagliatelle with vegetables and ham

Rigatoni with Borlotti Beans

INGREDIENTS *serves 4*

3½ cups rigatoni (or macaroni)
salt
2 tbsp olive oil
2 tbsp butter
1 clove garlic, crushed
14oz can borlotti beans, drained
1½ cups mozzarella cheese, diced
chopped parsley
freshly ground black pepper

PREPARATION

Put the pasta in a deep pot and pour over enough boiling water to just cover. Add a pinch of salt and a few drops of the oil, cover and cook on full power for 10 minutes. Leave covered.

Put the remaining oil in a bowl with the butter and cook on full power for 1 minute. Add the garlic and cook on full power for 1 minute. Stir in the borlotti beans and cook on full power for 2 minutes.

Drain the pasta and stir in the bean mixture and cheese. Cover and cook on full power for 1½ minutes, until the mozzarella begins to melt.

Sprinkle with chopped parsley and serve. Offer black pepper at the table.

Right: Rigatoni with borlotti beans

Penne with Golden Raisins and Pine Nuts

INGREDIENTS *serves 4*

14oz penne (pasta quills)
salt
3 tbsp olive oil
1 clove garlic, chopped
3 tbsp golden raisins, plumped up in a little marsala
¼ cup pine nuts
3 tbsp finely chopped fennel leaves
grated Parmesan cheese
freshly ground black pepper

PREPARATION

Put the penne in a bowl and pour on enough boiling water to cover. Add a pinch of salt and a few drops of oil, cover and cook on full power for 9 minutes. Set aside, covered, while you prepare the sauce.

Put the olive oil in a dish and cook on full power for 30 seconds. Add the garlic and cook on full power for 1 minute. Stir in the golden raisins and pine nuts and cook on full power for 2 minutes, stirring once during that time.

Drain the pasta, pour on the sauce, add the fennel and toss well.

Serve with plenty of freshly grated Parmesan cheese and offer freshly ground black pepper at the table.

Spaghetti with Ricotta *and* Almonds

INGREDIENTS *serves 4*

14oz spaghetti

4½ cups boiling water (approx)

salt

oil

¾ cup ground almonds

⅔ cup ricotta cheese

⅔ cup light cream

a pinch of sweet baking spice

slivered toasted almonds

Parmesan cheese

PREPARATION

A delicious and very unusual combination of tastes.

Hold the spaghetti in a deep pot and pour the water over it. As it softens, push the spaghetti under the water. Add a pinch of salt and a few drops of oil, cover and cook on full power for 12 minutes. Let the pot stand, covered, while you make the sauce.

Blend together the ground almonds, ricotta cheese and cream. Stir in the sweet baking spice to taste. Cover and heat through on medium power for 3 minutes.

Drain the pasta and stir in the sauce.

Sprinkle with slivered toasted almonds and serve hot with plenty of Parmesan cheese.

Right: Spaghetti with ricotta and almonds

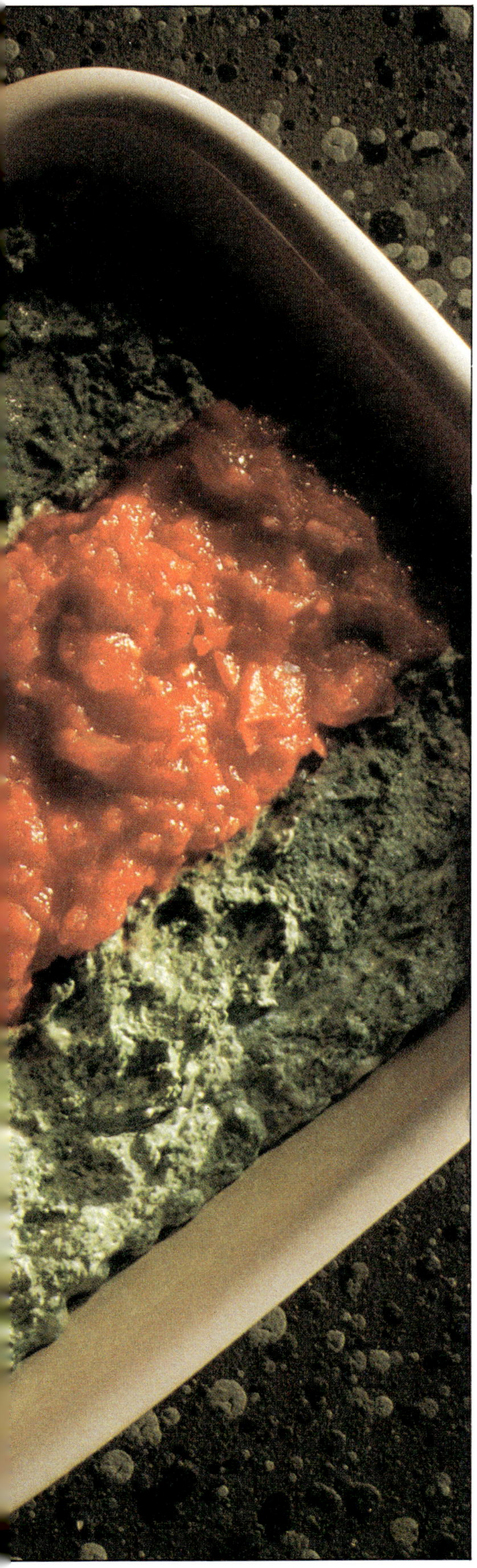

Lasagne with Spinach

INGREDIENTS *serves 4*
10-12 sheets lasagne
salt
2lb fresh spinach
¾ cup cream
8oz ricotta cheese
freshly ground black pepper
nutmeg
1tbsp oil
1 clove garlic, crushed
1 small onion, finely chopped
¾ cup canned tomatoes, strained

PREPARATION

Put the lasagne sheets in a deep oblong dish and cover with boiling water. Add a pinch of salt and a few drops of oil, cover and cook on full power for 10 minutes. Allow to stand, covered, while you make the sauces.

Wash the spinach and discard any tough stalks and discolored leaves. Put it in a boiling or roasting bag, with only the water clinging to it, tie loosely and cook on full power for 6 minutes. Drain and chop roughly.

Mix together the cream and ricotta cheese until well blended. Stir in the spinach and season with salt, black pepper and nutmeg to taste.

Assemble the lasagne in an oiled oblong dish. Layer the pasta and the spinach sauce until all are used up. Begin with a layer of pasta and end with a layer of sauce.

Make the tomato sauce. Put the oil in a bowl, add the onion and garlic and cook on full power for 2 minutes. Add the strained tomatoes and cook on full power for 2 minutes. Season to taste.

Pour the tomato sauce over the lasagne and heat through on medium power for 4-5 minutes. Serve hot.

Left: Lasagne with spinach

Pappardelle with Chicken Livers

INGREDIENTS *serves 4*
14oz pappardelle
salt
a few drops of oil
1tbsp olive oil
2 tbsp Marsala
2 shallots, finely chopped
1 clove garlic, finely chopped
1 cup chicken livers, trimmed and chopped
chopped parsley
lemon wedges

PREPARATION

Put the pappardelle in a deep pot and pour over enough boiling water to cover. Add a pinch of salt and a few drops of oil, cover and cook on full power for 9 minutes. Leave to stand, covered, while you prepare the pasta sauce.

Put the oil and Marsala in a dish with the shallots and garlic. Cover and cook on full power for 2 minutes. Stir in the chicken livers, and cook on full power for 2-3 minutes, stirring once, until just done.

Drain the pasta and top with the sauce. Sprinkle with chopped parsley and serve with lemon wedges.

Penne with Zucchini and Pistachio Nuts

INGREDIENTS *serves 4*
14oz penne (pasta quills)
salt
2-3tbsp olive oil
10oz baby zucchini, sliced
2 tbsp water
1 clove garlic, crushed
⅓ cup pistachio nuts, shelled
freshly ground black pepper
Parmesan cheese (optional)

PREPARATION

Put the penne in a deep pot and just cover with boiling water. Add a pinch of salt and a few drops of the oil, cover and cook on full power for 9 minutes. Set aside, covered.

Put the zucchini in a dish with the water, cover with vented plastic wrap and cook on full power for 3 minutes.

Put the olive oil in a dish and cook on full power for 30 seconds. Add the garlic and cook on full power for 1 minute. Drain the zucchini and add them with the pistachio nuts. Stir well to coat in the oil. Cover and cook on full power for 1-2 minutes.

Drain the pasta, pour over the sauce and season with black pepper. Offer Parmesan cheese at the table, if liked.

Right: Penne with zucchini and pistachio nuts

Spaghetti with Eggplant and Garlic

INGREDIENTS *serves 4*
14oz spaghetti
4½ cups boiling water
1 large eggplant
2-3tbsp olive oil
1-2 cloves garlic, crushed
Parmesan cheese (optional)

PREPARATION

Hold the spaghetti in a pot and pour on the boiling water. Push the spaghetti into it, add a few drops of oil and a little salt. Cover and cook on full power for 12 minutes.

Meanwhile, trim the eggplant and cut into thick matchsticks.

Remove the spaghetti from the microwave when it is ready and leave to stand, covered.

Put the olive oil in a dish and add the garlic and eggplant. Cover and cook on full power for 5 minutes, stirring once.

Drain the spaghetti and toss in the eggplant and garlic.

Serve with Parmesan cheese, if liked.

Tagliatelle with Anchovies and Tuna Fish

INGREDIENTS *serves 4*

2 tbsp olive oil
1 clove garlic, crushed
4 anchovy fillets, drained, soaked in milk, rinsed and chopped
½ cup canned tuna fish, drained
2 tbsp capers
⅓ cup black olives, pitted
14oz tagliatelle
salt
chopped parsley

PREPARATION

Put the oil in a bowl and add the garlic. Cook on full power for 1 minute. Stir in the anchovies, tuna, capers and olives, cover and cook on full power for 3 minutes.

Put the tagliatelle in a deep pot and just cover with boiling water. Add a pinch of salt and a few drops of oil, cover and cook on full power for 6 minutes. Let the pot stand for 3 minutes and reheat the sauce for 2 minutes while it is waiting.

Drain the pasta, pour over the sauce and garnish with chopped parsley.

Right: Tagliatelle with anchovies and tuna fish

Lasagne with Leeks *and* Sauce

INGREDIENTS *serves 4*
2 large leeks, sliced
8oz spicy sausage, sliced
$\frac{3}{4}$ cup strained tomatoes (passata)
a pinch dried mixed herbs
6 sheets spinach lasagne
a few drops of oil
3 tbsp butter
6 tbsp flour
$1\frac{1}{4}$ cups milk
$\frac{1}{2}$ cup grated cheese
salt and freshly ground black pepper
4 tbsp breadcrumbs

PREPARATION

Put the leeks and sausage in a deep oblong dish with 4 tbsp of the strained tomatoes (passata). Cover with vented plastic wrap and cook on full power for 6 minutes, stirring once. Add the rest of the strained tomato and the herbs, season, and set aside.

Put the lasagne in a deep pot and pour over enough boiling water to cover. Add a pinch of salt and a few drops of oil, cover and cook on full power for 15 minutes. Drain and rinse thoroughly under cold running water. Lay the pasta on a dish towel to dry. (Do not use paper towels.)

Make the cheese sauce. Put the butter in a dish and cook on full power for 1 minute. Stir in the flour. Pour on the milk. Cook on full power for 3 minutes, whisking after each minute. Stir in the cheese. Cook on full power for a further minute and whisk again. Season to taste.

Assemble the dish in layers until all the ingredients are used up, finishing with a layer of cheese sauce.

Top with breadcrumbs and heat through in the microwave or, if you would like the dish to brown, in a conventional oven or broiler. Serve hot.

Chicken Lasagne

INGREDIENTS *serves 4*
10-12 sheets lasagne
salt
oil
3 tbsp butter
1 onion, chopped
1 clove garlic, chopped
2 cups mushrooms, sliced
1 tsp dried oregano
6 tbsp flour
2 cups milk
1 chicken bouillon cube
1⅔ cups cooked chicken, chopped
4½ tbsp grated Parmesan cheese, plus extra for the topping

PREPARATION
Put the lasagne sheets in a deep oblong dish and cover with boiling water. Add a pinch of salt and a few drops of oil, cover and cook on full power for 10 minutes. Allow to stand, covered, while you make the sauce.

Put the butter in a bowl and cook on full power for 1 minute. Stir in the onion and garlic and cook on full power for 2 minutes. Stir in the mushrooms and oregano and cook on full power for 2 minutes.

Stir in the flour and gradually add the milk, stirring. Crumble on the bouillon cube. Cook on full power for 3 minutes, stirring after each minute. Stir in the chicken and cheese and cook on full power for 1 minute. Keep warm.

Drain the lasagne and lay the sheets out on a dish towel.

In an oiled oblong dish, layer the pasta and sauce until both are used up. Start with a layer of pasta and end with a layer of sauce. Sprinkle more Parmesan cheese on the top and cook on medium power for 5 minutes, turning the dish once. Serve hot.

Right: Chicken lasagne

Tagliatelle with Mussels and Shrimp

INGREDIENTS *serves 4*
1 tbsp olive oil
1 clove garlic, crushed
¾ cup canned tomatoes, drained and mashed
½ tsp dried basil, or fresh basil to taste, snipped
freshly ground black pepper
8oz peeled shrimp, plus a few unpeeled ones for garnish
14oz tagliatelle
salt
5 cups mussels, scrubbed clean
1 glass dry white wine
chopped parsley

PREPARATION
Put the oil in a bowl and cook on full power for 30 seconds. Add the garlic and cook on full power for 1 minute. Add the tomatoes, basil, pepper and peeled shrimp and cook on full power for 4 minutes. Season the mixture with salt to taste, set aside and keep warm.

Put the tagliatelle in a deep pot and pour over enough boiling water to just cover. Add a pinch of salt and a few drops of oil, cover and cook on full power for 6 minutes. Set aside, covered.

Discard any broken or open mussels and put the rest in a deep pot. Pour over the white wine. Add parsley to taste. Cover and cook on full power for 3 minutes, or until the mussels open.

Remove some mussels from their shells and stir into the sauce. Drain the pasta, pour over the sauce and garnish with the remaining mussels and the unpeeled shrimp.

Left: Tagliatelle with mussels and shrimp

Tagliatelle Bolognese

INGREDIENTS *serves 4*
1 tbsp oil
1 clove garlic, crushed
1 onion, finely chopped
1 carrrot, finely chopped
1 stick celery, finely chopped
¾ cup canned tomatoes, drained and mashed
7oz ground beef
⅓ cup ham
2 tbsp red wine
1 bay leaf
3 chicken livers, chopped
salt and freshly ground black pepper
14oz tagliatelle
Parmesan cheese

PREPARATION
Put the oil in a bowl and cook on full power for 30 seconds. Add the garlic, onion, carrot and celery and cook on full power for 2 minutes. Stir in the tomatoes, beef and ham and add the red wine to moisten. Tuck the bay leaf into the mixture. Cook on full power for 5 minutes, stirring once.

Add the chicken livers and cook on full power for 2 minutes. Season, set aside and keep warm.

Put the tagliatelle in a deep pot and pour over enough boiling water to just cover. Add a pinch of salt and a few drops of oil, cover and cook on full power for 6 minutes. Leave to stand, covered, for 3 minutes while you reheat the sauce if necessary.

Drain the pasta, pour over the sauce and serve with plenty of Parmesan cheese.

Left: Tagliatelle bolognese

Bucatini with Red *Lentil* Sauce

INGREDIENTS *serves 4*
1tbsp oil
1 onion, chopped
1 clove garlic, chopped
¾ cup canned tomatoes, drained and mashed
salt and freshly ground black pepper
scant cup red lentils
1¼ cups boiling water
3½ cups bucatini
Parmesan cheese

PREPARATION
Put the oil in a dish and cook on full power for 30 seconds. Add the onion and garlic, cover and cook on full power for 2 minutes. Add the tomatoes and seasoning. Set aside.

Put the lentils in a pot and pour over the boiling water. Cover and cook on full power for 12 minutes. Stir in the tomato sauce and set aside.

Put the bucatini in a deep pot. Cover with boiling water and add a few drops of oil. Cover and cook on full power for 9 minutes. Set aside while you reheat the sauce.

Drain the bucatini, stir in the sauce and serve topped with plenty of grated Parmesan cheese.

Stuffed Cannelloni

INGREDIENTS *serves 4*

1tbsp oil
1 onion, finely chopped
1 carrot, finely chopped
1 stick celery, finely chopped
2 tbsp red wine
1 tbsp tomato paste
7oz lean ground beef
7oz lean ground veal
⅔ cup ham, chopped
8oz cannelloni
3 tbsp butter
6 tbsp flour
1¼ cups milk
freshly ground black pepper
nutmeg
4½ tbsp Parmesan cheese, grated
1 egg yolk

PREPARATION

First make the stuffing. Put the oil in a bowl and cook on full power for 30 seconds. Stir in the onion, carrot and celery and cook on full power for 2 minutes. Stir in the wine mixed with the tomato paste. Add the beef, veal and ham and combine well. Cover and cook on full power for 5 minutes, until done. Season with salt and pepper.

Put the cannelloni in a deep oblong dish and just cover with boiling water. Add a pinch of salt and a few drops of oil. Cover and cook on full power for 9 minutes. Leave for 3 minutes, covered, then drain and stuff with the meat mixture.

Meanwhile, make the sauce. Put the butter in a bowl and cook on full power for 1 minute. Stir in the flour and cook on full power for 1 minute. Pour on the milk and cook on full power for 3 minutes, whisking after every minute. Add salt and pepper and a little nutmeg to taste. Stir in the grated Parmesan cheese and cook on full power for a further minute. Whisk again, then stir in the egg yolk.

Lay the stuffed cannelloni in a greased dish, in a single layer if possible. Pour over the sauce. Cover with vented plastic wrap and cook on full power for 1-2 minutes to heat through. Serve hot.

Right: Stuffed cannelloni

Linguine with Green Beans and Pumpkin Seeds

INGREDIENTS *serves 4*

8oz green beans, trimmed and cut into bite-sized pieces
2 tbsp water
¾ cup tomatoes, peeled, seeded and cut into strips
2oz pumpkin seeds
14oz green linguine
salt
1-2 tbsp oil
Parmesan cheese (optional)

PREPARATION

Put the beans in a dish with the water, cover with vented plastic wrap and cook on full power for 4 minutes.

Add the tomatoes and cook on full power for a further 4 minutes. Add the pumpkin seeds. Keep covered and keep warm.

Put the linguine in a deep pot with enough boiling water to cover. Add a pinch of salt and a few drops of oil. Cover and cook on full power for 8 minutes then set aside, covered.

Drain the vegetables and dress with the oil. Reheat, covered, for 1 minute.

Drain the pasta and mix in the dressed vegetables.

Serve with Parmesan cheese if liked.

Macaroni with Shrimp

INGREDIENTS *serves 4*
1tbsp oil
2 cloves garlic, crushed
1 red chili, seeded and chopped
14oz canned tomatoes, drained and mashed
1½ cups shelled shrimp
1tbsp lemon juice
freshly ground black pepper
a sprig of thyme
1 bay leaf
a few sprigs of parsley
3½ cups macaroni
salt
cucumber slices

PREPARATION
Put the oil in a bowl and cook on full power for 30 seconds. Add the garlic and chili and cook on full power for 1 minute. Stir in the tomatoes and cook for 3 minutes. Stir in the shrimp and lemon juice, sprinkle with black pepper and add the herbs. Cover and cook on full power for 2 minutes.

Put the macaroni in a bowl and just cover with boiling water. Add a pinch of salt and a few drops of oil, cover and cook on full power for 10 minutes. Leave to stand for 3 minutes. Reheat the sauce if necessary.

Drain the pasta and mix in the sauce.

Garnish with cucumber slices and serve piping hot.

Left: Macaroni with prawns (shrimp)

Spaghetti with Snow Peas

INGREDIENTS *serves 4*

1tbsp oil
2 tbsp butter
1 clove garlic, crushed
4oz snow peas, stalks removed
4oz button mushrooms, wiped and sliced
4oz fresh tomatoes, skinned and chopped
salt and freshly ground black pepper
14oz spaghetti
$4\frac{1}{2}$ cups boiling water
chopped fresh herbs
Parmesan cheese

PREPARATION

Put the oil in a bowl with the butter and cook on full power for 1 minute. Add the garlic and cook on full power for 1 minute. Stir in the snow peas, mushrooms and tomatoes. Cover with vented plastic wrap and cook on full power for 3 minutes. Season and set aside while you cook the pasta.

Hold the spaghetti in a deep pot. Pour over the boiling water and push the spaghetti down into the pot. Add a pinch of salt and a few drops of oil, cover and cook on full power for 12 minutes. Leave to stand, covered, for 5 minutes. Reheat the sauce during standing time if necessary.

Drain the pasta and top with the sauce. Sprinkle with fresh herbs and offer Parmesan cheese at the table.

Right: Spaghetti with snow peas

Farfalle al Gorgonzola

INGREDIENTS *serves 4*
6-8oz ripe Gorgonzola cheese
⅔ cup heavy or light cream
14oz farfalle (bow-shaped) pasta
salt
oil
freshly ground black pepper

PREPARATION
This is a luxurious dish that can be prepared very quickly.

If necessary, soften the cheese by putting it, wrapped, in the microwave for a few seconds on defrost power. Cream the cheese with the cream in the liquidizer. Put the mixture in a bowl and cook on full power for 2 minutes to warm through.

Put the pasta in a deep pot and just cover with boiling water. Add a pinch of salt and a few drops of oil, cover and cook on full power for 10 minutes. Leave to stand for 3 minutes.

Heat the sauce through again if necessary during the standing time. It should be warm, not hot.

Drain the pasta and stir in the sauce. Offer black pepper at the table.

Left: Farfalle al Gorgonzola

Bean-Stuffed Cannelloni

INGREDIENTS *serves 4*
2 cups canned cannellini beans, drained
⅔ cup ricotta cheese
1 bunch parsley, chopped
1 onion, chopped
¾ cup tomatoes, skinned, peeled and chopped
salt and freshly ground black pepper
8 cannelloni
a few drops of oil
⅔ cup light cream

PREPARATION
When cooked like this, the onion and tomato in the stuffing will still be crisp and firm respectively, which makes a refreshing change from the norm.

Make the stuffing by mixing together the beans, ricotta, parsley, onion and tomatoes, and season well with salt and pepper.

Put the cannelloni in a deep oblong dish and cover with boiling water. Add a few drops of oil and a pinch of salt. Cover and cook on full power for 12 minutes. Drain and rinse under cold running water.

Stuff the cannelloni with the bean mixture and arrange in the dish. Pour the cream over and reheat for 2 minutes. Serve at once while piping hot.

Green Tagliatelle with Peppers

INGREDIENTS *serves 4*
1tbsp olive oil
1 small onion, chopped
1 clove garlic, crushed
1½ cups canned tomatoes, drained
salt and freshly ground black pepper
½ red bell pepper, cut into strips about 1in long
½ green bell pepper, cut into strips about 1in long
½ yellow bell pepper, cut into strips about 1in long
2 tbsp water
14oz spinach tagliatelle
salt
Parmesan cheese

PREPARATION

Put the oil in a bowl and cook on full power for 30 seconds. Add the onion and garlic and cook on full power for 2 minutes. Purée in a liquidizer and season to taste.

Put the pepper strips in a bowl and add the water. Cover with vented plastic wrap and cook for 4 minutes, until tender. Set aside.

Put the tagliatelle in a deep pot and just cover with boiling water. Add a pinch of salt and a few drops of oil, cover and cook on full power for 6 minutes. Leave to stand for 3 minutes. Reheat the sauce if necessary during standing time.

Drain the pasta, pour over the sauce and garnish with the strips of pepper.

Serve with Parmesan cheese.

Right: Green tagliatelle with peppers

Rigatoni Country-Style

INGREDIENTS *serves 4*
14oz rigatoni (or macaroni)
salt
oil
6oz spicy sausage, cut into chunks or sliced
1½ cups cauliflower flowerets
1tbsp water
1 cup green beans, trimmed and cut into bite size pieces
1-2 tbsp olive oil
cayenne pepper
1 whole mozzarella cheese, diced

PREPARATION
Use the long spicy sausages sold in coils for this dish. If you can't find these sausages, use diced salami.

Put the rigatoni in a deep pot and just cover with boiling water. Add a pinch of salt and a few drops of oil. Cover and cook on full power for 10 minutes. Leave to stand, covered, while you make the sauce.

Put the sausage pieces on a plate covered with absorbent paper towels and cook on full power for 1½ minutes. Cover, set aside and keep warm.

Put the cauliflower in a bowl with the water. Cover and cook on full power for 1 minute. Add the beans, cover and cook on full power for 3 minutes.

Drain the pasta and vegetables. Pour the olive oil over the pasta and season with cayenne pepper. Stir in the cauliflower, beans, sausage and diced mozzarella cheese, cover and heat through for 1 minute. Serve while piping hot.

Left: Rigatoni country-style

Lasagne and Ham Rolls

INGREDIENTS *serves 4*
4 sheets spinach lasagne
salt
oil
4 slices ham, the same size as the lasagne sheets

PREPARATION
This makes a tasty and attractive appetizer and it is also an unusual accompaniment to drinks. It is simple to prepare, but looks extremely elegant.

Put the lasagne in a deep pot with enough boiling water to cover. Add a pinch of salt and a few drops of oil. Cover and cook on full power for 10 minutes. Leave to stand for 3 minutes. Drain and rinse well under cold running water.

Lay the lasagne sheets out on a dish towel to dry. Do not use paper towels – they will stick to the pasta.

When the lasagne has cooled, lay a slice of ham on top of each sheet and roll the lasagne up tightly.

Cut each roll into slices and serve cold.

Linguine with Mushroom Sauce

INGREDIENTS *serves 4*
8oz mushrooms, wiped and sliced
2 tbsp milk
14oz green linguine
salt
oil
⅔ cup light cream
chopped parsley

PREPARATION
Put the mushrooms in a dish and add the milk. Cover and cook on full power for 3 minutes, stirring once. Set aside, covered.

Put the linguine in a deep pot and pour over enough boiling water to cover. Add a pinch of salt and a few drops of oil. Cover and cook on full power for 9 minutes. Set aside, covered.

Stir the cream into the mushrooms. Reheat for 1 minute.

Drain the pasta, pour on the mushrooms, garnish with parsley and serve.

Tagliatelle with Peas and Cream

INGREDIENTS *serves 4*
14oz tagliatelle
salt
oil
⅔ cup heavy cream
3½ cups cooked peas or use frozen and defrosted peas
½ cup Emmenthal cheese, grated
⅓ cup Parmesan cheese, grated
strips of pepper

PREPARATION
Put the tagliatelle in a pot and pour over enough boiling water to just cover. Add a pinch of salt and a few drops of oil, cover and cook on full power for 6 minutes. Leave to stand, covered.

Pour the cream into a bowl and stir in the peas. Cook on full power for 1½ minutes. Stir in both cheeses and cook on full power for 1½ minutes, stirring twice, until melted.

Drain the tagliatelle, stir in the sauce and serve immediately garnished with the strips of pepper.

Right: Tagliatelle with peas and cream

Pasta Shells with Crab Meat

INGREDIENTS *serves 4*
14oz pasta shells
salt
oil
1 scant cup crab meat, flaked
$^{2}/_{3}$ cup light cream
1 tbsp marsala
cayenne pepper
chopped parsley

PREPARATION
Put the pasta shells in a deep pot, just cover with boiling water, add a pinch of salt and a few drops of oil, cover and cook on full power for 9 minutes. Allow to stand, covered, while you make the sauce.

Stir the crab meat into the cream, add the marsala and cook on full power for 3 minutes.

Drain the pasta, stir in the sauce, sprinkle with cayenne pepper and garnish with chopped parsley.

Right: Pasta shells with crab meat

Rigatoni with Sardines

INGREDIENTS *serves 4*
14oz rigatoni
salt
1 tbsp oil
1 clove garlic, crushed
5oz canned sardines in tomato sauce
4 leaves fresh sage, chopped
freshly ground black pepper

PREPARATION

Put the rigatoni in a dish and cover with boiling water. Add a pinch of salt and a few drops of the oil, cover and cook on full power for 9 minutes. Leave to stand, covered, while you prepare the sauce.

Put the remaining oil in a bowl and cook on full power for 30 seconds. Add the garlic and cook on full power for $1\frac{1}{2}$ minutes.

Mash the sardines in their tomato sauce and add to the bowl. Cover and cook on full power for 2–3 minutes, stirring once, until hot through.

Drain the pasta, pour the sardine and tomato sauce over it, sprinkle with fresh sage and pepper and serve.

Tagliatelle with Spinach and Walnut Sauce

INGREDIENTS *serves 4*

1lb fresh spinach
4 strips bacon, trimmed and chopped
½oz butter
1 clove garlic, crushed
⅔ cup light cream
⅓ cup walnut pieces
14oz tagliatelle
salt
oil
Parmesan cheese

PREPARATION

Wash the spinach and discard any tough leaves and stalks. Put it into a roasting or boiling bag with only the water clinging to it, tie loosely and cook on full power for 6 minutes, until the leaves have collapsed. Purée the spinach in a blender.

Put the bacon on a plate covered with absorbent paper towels and cook on full power for 2 minutes until done.

Put the butter in a small bowl with the garlic, add the bacon and cook on full power for 2 minutes.

Stir the spinach into the cream, add the walnuts and cook on full power for 4 minutes. Set aside, covered.

Put the tagliatelle in a deep bowl and just cover with boiling water. Add a pinch of salt and a few drops of oil and cook on full power for 6 minutes. Let the bowl stand, covered, while you reheat the spinach cream sauce if necessary.

Drain the pasta and stir in the cream sauce. Top with the garlic and bacon. Serve hot with Parmesan cheese.

Left: Tagliatelle with spinach and walnut sauce.

Pasta and Ham Salad

INGREDIENTS *serves 4*
14oz shell pasta
salt
a few drops of oil
$^2/_3$ cup diced ham
2 cups cooked lima beans (or use canned beans, drained)
$^2/_3$ cup sour cream
freshly ground black pepper
mint leaves

PREPARATION
Put the pasta in a dish and pour over enough boiling water to cover. Add a pinch of salt and a few drops of oil, cover and cook on full power for 9 minutes. Rinse under cold running water and drain thoroughly.

Toss the pasta with the ham and lima beans in the sour cream. Season with salt and pepper and garnish attractively with mint leaves.

Pasta with Garbanzo Beans

INGREDIENTS *serves 4*
14oz multi-colored pasta
salt
1 tbsp oil
2 tbsp butter
1 clove garlic, crushed
2 cups canned garbanzo beans, drained
$^1/_3$-$^1/_2$ cup freshly grated Parmesan cheese
freshly ground black pepper

PREPARATiON
This is a very simple dish called "thunder and lightning" in Italy. Make it with canned garbanzo beans to save time.

Put the pasta in a bowl and just cover with boiling water. Add a pinch of salt and a few drops of oil, cover and cook on full power for 10 minutes. Allow to stand, covered.

Put the butter in a bowl and cook on full power for 1 minute. Stir in the garlic and garbanzo beans, cover and cook for 2 minutes.

Drain the pasta. Pour over the oil and the garlic garbanzo beans and add the Parmesan cheese.

Stir and serve at once. Offer black pepper at the table.

Right: Pasta with chickpeas (garbanzos)

SAUCES

Most people enjoy pasta with sauce and the more unusual sauces as well as the old favorites, served with different pastas, can add endless variety to everyday meals. The Italians are known for their use of fresh young vegetables and it is the fresh ingredients that make even the most simple sauce, served with well cooked pasta, a feast. When preparing sauces with vegetables, it is as well to remember to serve pasta of a similar size to that of the sauce ingredients. It is difficult to pick up small pasta with chunky vegetables.

Béchamel Sauce

INGREDIENTS *makes 2½ cups*
2½ cups milk
1 small onion, peeled
1 small carrot, peeled and sliced
1 bay leaf
6 slightly crushed peppercorns
1 blade of mace
1 stalk parsley
3 tbsp butter
6 tbsp flour
salt and white pepper

PREPARATION
Pour the milk into a saucepan. Add the onion cut into quarters with two slices of carrot, the bay leaf, peppercorns, mace and parsley stalk.

Cover and allow to heat on a low heat without boiling for about 10 minutes. Remove from the heat and allow to infuse for a further 10 minutes, covered.

Make a roux (a blend of butter and flour) by melting the butter in a saucepan. Do not allow the butter to brown. Add the flour and stir well over a medium heat.

Gradually add the strained milk and stir briskly or whisk until a smooth creamy sauce is made. Season to taste.

Page 120: Béchamel sauce

Tuna and Mushroom Sauce

INGREDIENTS *makes $1\frac{7}{8}$ cups*
2 tbsp butter
1 tbsp oil
4oz mushrooms, washed
generous 1 cup canned tuna fish
2 tsp tomato paste
2 tbsp white wine
$2\frac{1}{2}$ cups Béchamel Sauce (page 122)
salt and freshly ground pepper

PREPARATION

Heat the butter and oil and cook the mushrooms for 3 minutes, turning from time to time.

Flake the tuna fish. Add the tomato paste and white wine to the Béchamel Sauce. Mix well.

Over a low heat, re-heat the sauce and gradually stir in the tuna fish and the drained mushrooms. Cook gently for a few minutes until well mixed and hot. Taste and adjust seasoning.

Mix the sauce with 1lb cooked pasta such as tagliatelle.

Mornay Sauce

INGREDIENTS *makes 3 cups*
2 egg yolks
2 tbsp cream
$2\frac{1}{2}$ cups Béchamel Sauce (page 122)
$\frac{1}{3}$ cup grated Parmesan cheese

PREPARATION

Mix the egg yolks with the cream and add a little warm Béchamel. Return to the warm Béchamel Sauce and stir well.

Lastly fold in the grated cheese.

Left: Tuna and mushroom sauce

Blue Cheese Sauce

INGREDIENTS *makes 1⅞ cups*
2½ cups Béchamel Sauce (page 122)
⅔ cup Roquefort or other blue cheese
salt and freshly ground pepper
½ tsp French mustard
pinch of cayenne pepper

PREPARATION
Make up the Béchamel Sauce. Crumble the blue cheese and add it to the sauce. Stir over a low heat.

Taste for seasoning. Add salt and pepper to taste and then the mustard. Lastly stir in the pinch of cayenne.

This sauce is sufficient to accompany approximately 3-4 cups/1-1½lb cooked pasta.

Ricotta

Ricotta is a moist curd cheese made from sheep's milk and can be either mild or strong, according to region. In Piedmont and around Rome it is eaten very fresh with pepper and salt, or sometimes with coffee and sugar sprinkled on it. It can be used in cooking sweet and savory dishes. In southern Italy ricotta forte is made from salted sheep's milk. It can be dried in the sun or in an oven and grated for cooking.

Spinach and Ricotta Sauce

INGREDIENTS *makes approximately 2½ cups*
1¼ cups Béchamel Sauce (page 122)
½ cup (after cooking) fresh or frozen spinach
⅔ cup ricotta cheese
½ tsp nutmeg
salt and freshly ground pepper

PREPARATION
Make up the béchamel sauce. Cook the spinach for a few minutes and then drain well. Squeeze against the colander to remove the liquid.

You will need to cook approx 1½lb fresh spinach to be left with the amount required by the recipe. Chop or liquidize.

Mix the ricotta with the spinach and season well, then add the nutmeg. Gradually stir into the béchamel sauce and re-heat carefully over a low heat.

Serve with approximately 3-4 cups/1-1½lb cooked pasta.

This sauce is also delicious used in a vegetable or chicken lasagne.

Right: Spinach and ricotta sauce

Tomato Sauce

INGREDIENTS *makes 2½ cups*

2 tbsp oil
1 large onion, peeled and diced
1-2 cloves garlic, peeled and crushed
2 sticks celery, washed
1 carrot, scraped and grated
1½ cups canned tomatoes
1lb fresh tomatoes, skinned and chopped
1 bouquet garni
1 bay leaf
1 tbsp fresh or ½tsp dried basil, chopped
1 stalk parsley
½ tsp sugar
1¼ cups chicken or beef stock
2 tbsp red wine
salt and freshly ground pepper

PREPARATION

Heat the oil in a saucepan and cook the onions over a low heat for 5 minutes until transparent. Add the garlic to the onions.

Remove the strings from the celery with a sharp knife and chop into small pieces. Add to the onion.

Add all the other ingredients, bring to a boil, lower the heat and simmer for 40 minutes. Remove the bouquet garni, bay leaf and parsley stalk and serve with pasta.

For a smooth-textured sauce pass through a strainer or blender.

Tomato Sauce II

INGREDIENTS *serves 4*

1 onion, peeled and finely chopped
2 cloves garlic, crushed
1 carrot, scraped and grated
2 tbsp freshly chopped parsley
1 tbsp freshly chopped basil
1 bay leaf
3lb large tomatoes, skinned and chopped
4 tbsp dry white wine

PREPARATION

Place all the ingredients in a thick saucepan and simmer for 20 minutes until the tomatoes are puréed.

Strain the sauce or pass through an electric blender or food processor. Taste for seasoning and adjust.

This fresh tomato sauce is really best made with large ripe beefsteak tomatoes and fresh basil. The taste with fresh pasta is truly delicious.

Right: Ravioli makes a mouthwatering first course whether served steaming hot in a cooked tomato sauce or chilled in a thick salsa of strained and herbed fresh tomato pulp.

Tomato Sauce III

INGREDIENTS *serves 4*

4 tbsp olive oil
2 cloves garlic, crushed
4½ cups ripe beefsteak tomatoes, peeled and chopped
salt and freshly ground pepper
6 basil leaves

PREPARATION

Heat the oil in a saucepan, add the garlic and stir for 1 minute. Add the tomatoes and seasoning and allow the sauce to simmer for 6 minutes.

Chop the basil leaves and add to the tomatoes, stir the sauce for a further minute. Serve on freshly cooked pasta.

This sauce is a simple accompaniment to pasta which is very good to eat and easy to prepare but the secret is that the tomatoes should be simply heated through, not cooked to a pulp.

Piquant Tomato Sauce

INGREDIENTS *serves 4*

2¾lb firm, ripe tomatoes
4 medium green bell peppers
1 small red bell pepper
1 pickled pepper
¾ cup sliced onions
2 whole cloves
1 cinnamon stick
1 bay leaf
salt
1 cup white wine vinegar
2 tbsp sugar
olive oil

PREPARATION

This sauce is similar to tomato ketchup and makes a good accompaniment to roast and boiled meats and hard-boiled eggs.

Halve and seed the tomatoes, place in a large pan (not an aluminum pan). Halve and seed the bell peppers and add to the tomatoes. Add the pickled pepper, onions, cloves, cinnamon stick, bay leaf and 1 teaspoon salt. Stir well and simmer for 3 hours over very low heat. Make sure condensation on the pan lid does not drip into the sauce. Use a cloth or paper towels to soak it up when you lift lid.

After 3 hours, remove the pan from the heat and rub the mixture through a strainer, discarding the cloves, bay leaf and cinnamon stick. Return to the pan, add vinegar and sugar and simmer over very low heat for about 2 hours.

Cool the sauce, then pour into five small jars; cover the sauce in each jar with about ¼in oil. Add lids and store the sauce in the refrigerator.

Tomato And Meat Sauce

INGREDIENTS *makes 9lb sauce*

8lb firm, ripe tomatoes
1lb slender carrots
¾ cup sliced celery
½ cup mixed chopped parsley, sage and basil
5 cloves garlic, crushed
1lb onions, thinly sliced
¼ cup butter
⅓ cup olive oil
1¾lb lean ground beef
salt

PREPARATION

Cook the tomato sauce by putting the tomatoes, carrots, celery, herbs and garlic in a large pan. Heat gently and when they have reached simmering point cover and cook for 2½ hours, stirring occasionally.

Put the onions in a pan with butter and olive oil. Heat gently until softened, add the meat and cook for 1½ hours, adding a little tomato juice if necessary. Combine the meat sauce with the tomato sauce and cook for 1 hour longer, then season with salt.

This sauce can be frozen or canned.

Hot Anchovy Dip

INGREDIENTS *serves 4*
1/2 cup flat anchovy fillets
5 cloves garlic
2 tbsp butter
3/4 cup virgin olive oil
salt

PREPARATION
This hot dip is a speciality of Piedmont. It is brought to the table in a terracotta saucepan and put over a little candle – if possible each person should have his or her own chafing dish. Each person dips crudités or cooked vegetables into the sauce. Use tender white cardoons – a relative of the thistle and the artichoke – soaked first in acidulated cold water; peppers, celery, tender cauliflower etc, or cooked onions, potatoes, beets, carrots and turnips, etc. Make sure the dish is stable to avoid accidents.

If you want the garlic to be more digestible, soak it for 2 hours in a glass of milk before use. In some parts of Piedmont it is customary to add crushed pieces of walnut to the dip. Leftovers of the sauce can be served with scrambled eggs.

Rinse the anchovies well, then pat dry. Cut the garlic into fine slivers or, if preferred, crush it. Put the pan over a low flame and add the butter and garlic. Let it cook gently for a few minutes without browning, then gradually add the oil and the anchovies. Blend the anchovies in well and cook over a very low flame for about 15 minutes, stirring occasionally. Finally taste and add salt, if necessary. Serve in the cooking dish.

Anchovies

Anchovies are used in cooking all over Italy. You can buy anchovy fillets canned in oil, anchovy paste and anchovy essence, but these are no real substitute for anchovies prepared at home. Whole salt-cured anchovies are sometimes available from Cypriot or Greek delicatessens, as well as specialist Italian shops. They are sold loose in a drum and should be filleted and steeped in oil as soon as possible.

Rinse the anchovies well in cold running water. Cover the work surface or a board with waxed paper, lay the fish on it and scrape off the skin. Remove the dorsal fin and the bones joined to it. Separate the fish into two halves with a knife and remove the spine. Lay the fillets in a shallow dish and cover each layer with olive oil. Make sure the top layer is completely submerged in oil. Store for up to two weeks in the fridge.

Tomatoes

Though an indispensable ingredient in Italian cooking, the tomato was introduced into the country only comparatively recently. The Italians grow either plum tomatoes or the huge, curved, irregular Marmande variety – both have infinitely more flavor than the pale, insipid specimens cultivated in Britain and America. Many Italians bottle their own tomatoes and make their own tomato concentrate at home for use during the winter months. Those who have neither the time nor the space use the canned variety.

Salsa Verde

This sharp green sauce is often served with boiled meats and with white fish. Use vinegar for a meat sauce and lemon juice for a fish one. Blend together 1/4 cup olive oil and 1 tbsp each of parsley and capers, 2 anchovy fillets, 1/2 clove garlic and 1 tsp either red wine vinegar or lemon juice.

Pepper Sauce

INGREDIENTS *makes 2 1/2 cups*
1 red bell pepper, seeded
1 green bell pepper, seeded
1 tbsp chopped parsley
1 1/4 cups tomato sauce, liquidized

PREPARATION
Dice the seeded peppers quite fine. Add to the liquidized tomato sauce with 4 tbsp stock or water and simmer for 10 minutes.

Add chopped parsley and use either alone with pasta or alternatively with meat or fish accompanying pasta.

Ragu Sauce

INGREDIENTS *serves 4*

1 onion, peeled
2 cloves garlic, crushed
1 carrot, scraped and grated
1 stick celery
6 tomatoes, peeled and chopped or $1\frac{1}{2}$ cups canned tomatoes
4 tbsp oil
1 cup lean ground beef
$\frac{1}{2}$ cup chicken livers
1 bouquet garni
1 bay leaf
$1\frac{1}{4}$ cups stock and red wine
1 tsp oregano
1 stalk parsley

PREPARATION

Prepare the vegetables. Cut the onion finely, coarsely grate the carrot. Wash the celery and remove strings with a sharp knife before chopping into very small pieces. Prepare the tomatoes.

Heat half the oil in a saucepan and cook the onion and garlic for 3 minutes over a low heat. Add the carrot and celery, stir into the oil and allow to cook for a further 3 minutes.

Heat the remaining oil in a skillet and brown the beef well over a high heat. Turn the heat down to medium and add the chopped chicken livers. Mix with the beef and cook until brown.

Add the meat to the vegetables with the herbs and wine, season well, add the stock and simmer for 45 minutes. Taste for seasoning before serving with freshly cooked pasta.

Bolognese Sauce

INGREDIENTS *serves 4*

1 large onion, peeled and diced
1 carrot, scraped and grated
1 stick celery, washed and chopped
2 cloves garlic, crushed
2 slices bacon
1 tbsp oil
4oz lean ground beef
4oz lean ground veal
1¼ cups beef stock or water
1½ cups canned tomatoes
4 tomatoes, skinned and chopped
1 bay leaf
1 tsp oregano
½ tsp basil
1 bouquet garni
salt and freshly ground pepper
1 tbsp tomato paste
⅝ cup red wine

PREPARATION

Prepare the vegetables, making sure that they are diced very fine. Remove the strings from the celery with a sharp knife before chopping. Cut the bacon into small pieces, having first removed the rind.

Heat the oil in the pan and brown all the meat over a medium heat. Remove with a slotted spoon, leaving any fat behind. Cook the vegetables in the meat fat, adding a little extra oil if necessary, over a low heat for 5 minutes.

Put the meat and vegetables into a saucepan with the tomatoes, herbs and seasoning. Lastly add the tomato paste and stir in the wine.

Bring to a boil and simmer gently for 45 minutes. Remove the bouquet garni and bay leaf before serving.

Serve with spaghetti and other pastas with Parmesan cheese served separately.

Right: Bolognese sauce

Capers

Capers are the small, green, unripe fruit of a climbing plant and have a very individual flavor. They are sold pickled in vinegar. If the vinegar is too strong, you may have to rinse the capers in water before use. Capers are much used in sauces for pasta, meat and fish.

Herbs

There is no doubt that fresh herbs have much to add to the flavors we create in the kitchen. As it is possible to buy potted herbs from garden centers and packets of fresh herbs from many supermarkets and vegetable shops, it is worth the effort to cook with fresh herbs.

Many of the herbs so characteristic of Italian cooking were originally used by the Romans medicinally as well as in the cooking pot. With the increasing interest in fresh food and healthy diets, most people are also more aware of the value and taste of fresh herbs. It is worth cultivating your own as they are decorative and edible. Many urban gardeners grow their own herbs very successfully, even on window-sills and balconies, and it is certainly interesting to try. Here are a few which grow in town most successfully and which are indispensable in pasta and pizza cooking. Dried herbs are inevitably necessary at certain times of the year and they make quite acceptable substitutes; it is best to buy them in small quantities as and when you need them. A jar of dried herbs which has been in the cupboard for over a year will not have much flavor remaining.

Putanesca Sauce

INGREDIENTS *makes 2½ cups*
1 onion, peeled and diced
2 tbsp oil
1 carrot, scraped and chopped
1½ cups canned tomatoes
2 tomatoes, skinned and chopped
4 tbsp white wine
1 bay leaf
3-4 basil leaves or 1tsp dried basil
salt and freshly ground pepper
1 tbsp capers, chopped
1 small can anchovies
½ cup pitted black olives
3 drops Tabasco sauce
1 tbsp freshly chopped parsley

PREPARATION
Put the onion into the oil in a skillet over a low heat. Allow to cook gently for 4 minutes, then add the crushed garlic and carrots. Turn in the oil for another minute, add the tomatoes, the white wine, bay leaf, basil, some seasoning and 4 anchovy fillets. Bring to a boil and simmer for 30 minutes. Strain or liquidize into a measuring jug. Return to the saucepan and add chopped capers, the remainder of the anchovies chopped into small pieces, chopped olives and the spicy Tabasco sauce. Re-heat gently.

Serve with 1lb cooked pasta with Parmesan cheese served separately.

Mayonnaise

INGREDIENTS *makes 1 1/4 cups*

2 egg yolks
1 1/4 cups olive oil
1/2 tsp salt
pinch of white pepper
pinch of dried mustard
1 tbsp wine vinegar or lemon juice

PREPARATION

Make sure the eggs are used at room temperature and not taken directly from the refrigerator. Warm a clean dry bowl slightly for the egg yolks, mix for a few seconds. Gradually add the oil, drop by drop to begin with. Mix briskly with a wooden spoon or a small wire whisk. The mixture will become a thick creamy emulsion as the drops of oil are added. When the mixture has thickened add the seasoning with vinegar or lemon juice. Beat well. The mayonnaise can be made thicker or thinner according to the amount of vinegar or lemon juice used. Taste for seasoning before using.

Note: To mix with pasta, a little more lemon juice may be used, as a thinner sauce is better for coating the cooked pasta.

Chef's tips

The process in making mayonnaise is a chemical one known as "emulsification," in which individual molecules of one liquid are held in suspension by another, in this case the oil and egg yolks respectively.

Work with ingredients at room temperature, never straight from the fridge.

Do not exceed the 2 yolks to 1 1/4 cups oil relationship. This is all the oil the eggs can "hold."

Go slowly with the oil until you're used to the process. The eggs need a little coaxing to start with.

Below: Fresh basil provides a brilliant green color and an inimitable flavor. If it is not available, parsley will provide a green sauce with quite a different emphasis.

Winter Pesto Sauce

INGREDIENTS *makes 1 1/4 cups*

1/2 cup fresh parsley
2 cloves garlic
1/2 cup pine nuts
1/3 cup Parmesan cheese
salt and freshly ground pepper
2 tsp dried basil
5/8 cup olive oil

PREPARATION

Chop the parsley finely in the blender or with a sharp knife if making by hand. Add the garlic to the blender and process for a few seconds. Gradually add the other ingredients through the top of the machine while it is running. When the mixture is puréed add a little olive oil at a time. Add the dried basil when half the oil has been added. Continue adding oil until a thick creamy mixture is made.

To make by hand see instructions for Genoese Pesto Sauce (left).

Genoese Pesto Sauce

INGREDIENTS *makes $1\frac{1}{4}$ cups*
2 tbsp fresh basil leaves
2 cloves garlic
pinch of salt
$\frac{1}{2}$ cup pine nuts
$\frac{1}{3}$ cup Parmesan cheese
$\frac{1}{2}$ cup olive oil

PREPARATION
Blend the basil leaves in a liquidizer. Add the crushed cloves of garlic and olive oil. Process for a few seconds. Gradually add the pine nuts and Parmesan cheese. Season, remembering that Parmesan has a salty taste. The consistency should be thick and creamy.

Note: This sauce was originally made by grinding the basil with the garlic salt and pine nuts in a pestle and mortar into a purée. Add the cheese and the oil gradually.

Even in summer it is not always easy to obtain a great deal of basil and although the flavor is different, fresh parsley and basil together can be substituted.

This quantity of pesto will be sufficient for 1lb cooked drained pasta. Melt 2 tbsp butter in the saucepan and re-heat the cooked pasta. Remove from the heat and mix 2 tbsp pesto with the pasta. Serve on individual plates with a spoonful of pesto on each helping. Parmesan can be added last.

The pesto is never heated. It can be served on pasta at the table but make sure the pasta is hot when served.

Pine Nuts

These come from the cones of the stone pine and are usually available from health food stores and delicatessens. They are small and creamy colored with a sweet, delicate flavor. They are used in pesto and sweet and sour (agrodolce) sauces as well as in sweet cakes and cookies.

Olive Oil

Olive oil is the major cooking medium around the Ligurian coast, in Tuscany and southern Italy. The best oil is said to come from Lucca in Tuscany. The first pressing of the olives produces a rich, fruity, green oil that is preferred by the cognoscenti to the mellower, more golden variety produced later on. Sadly, oil for export is often blended for uniformity and much of its character is lost.

Buy the most expensive olive oil you can afford for use on salads and in cooking dishes where its strong flavor is a component part of the dish. Where the flavor would be obtrusive, substitute a cheaper tasteless oil such as peanut oil. The very best olive oil is too good and too expensive to be used indiscriminately.

Right: 1. Olive oil which is widely used as a salad oil; 2. fine olive oil which is ideal for frying; 3. extra virgin olive oil which is the best for salads.

RICE

An Italian risotto is tender and moist, not dry, unlike the rice dishes of India and the Middle East. Serve it in soup plates, sprinkled with plenty of Parmesan cheese.

Chicken Risotto

INGREDIENTS *serves 4*

3lb chicken, cooked, giblets reserved
$^2/_3$ cup chopped veal
1 carrot, chopped
1 onion, chopped
1 stick celery, chopped
salt
$^1/_2$ cup butter
pepper
1 cup dry white wine
3 medium tomatoes, chopped
1$^1/_2$ cups rice
4 tbsp grated Parmesan cheese

PREPARATION

Skin and bone the chicken; dice the flesh and set aside. Put the veal, chicken bones and giblets into a pan with half the carrot, onion and celery. Cover with water, add a pinch of salt and cook over medium heat for about 30 minutes. Strain this stock, set aside and keep hot.

In a second pan, lightly brown the remaining chopped vegetables in half the butter. Add the diced chicken, season with salt and pepper and continue cooking, covered, for a few minutes. Pour in the wine, reduce by half, add the tomatoes and cook until soft.

Pour in the rice and add a ladleful of the stock. Continue adding stock at intervals as the rice dries out. When it is cooked, remove from the heat, stir in the remaining butter and half the Parmesan. Allow to stand for a minute and then serve with the remaining Parmesan cheese.

Page 134: Risotto with two cheeses

Risotto with Two Cheeses

INGREDIENTS *serves 4*

4 tbsp butter
1 medium onion, finely sliced
1$^2/_3$ cups Arborio (risotto) rice
2 chicken bouillon cubes or 3$^3/_4$ cups Pastine in Brodo (see page 56)
$^1/_2$ cup fresh grated Parmesan cheese
$^2/_3$ cup heavy cream
$^1/_2$ cup crumbled Gorgonzola
salt and freshly grated black pepper to taste

PREPARATION

Melt the butter in a sturdy pan and soften the onion in it. Add the rice and toast it for 2-3 minutes.

Crumble in the bouillon and add 3$^3/_4$ cups water. Cook the rice until it is *al dente*. Add the Parmesan.

As the rice is cooking, warm the cream and add the crumbled Gorgonzola to it. Stir until the cheese has thoroughly melted.

When the rice is cooked, whisk in the cream and Gorgonzola, season and serve while piping hot.

Above: Chicken risotto

Above: Risotto with dried ceps

Ceps

In the fall, Italians go mushroom hunting for *porcini* (ceps) which are very fleshy and can be served instead of a meat course. Strict laws govern the quantity and size of mushrooms a person may pick, and anyone finding a fungus of dubious species may have it checked by the authorities. Many different varieties of mushroom grow wild – the market at Trento sells 230 species. Mushrooms not eaten fresh can be dried for use during the rest of the year. Dried mushrooms should be soaked in warm water for a few minutes and not be cooked too long in a dish or they will lose their flavor.

Risotto with Dried Ceps

INGREDIENTS *serves 4-6*

2oz dried ceps
1¼ cups dry white wine
1 chicken bouillon cube or 4¼ cups Pastine in Brodo (see page 56)
1 small onion
¼ cup olive oil
2 cups Arborio (risotto) rice
⅔ cup heavy cream
3 tbsp freshly grated Parmesan cheese
salt and freshly grated black pepper to taste

PREPARATION

Put the dried ceps in a pot and cover them with the dry white wine. Crumble the bouillon cube over them and add 4¼ cups water.

Poach the ceps gently in the stock and wine until they are soft and swollen. Strain them carefully and reserve the poaching liquid. Wash the ceps once or twice more in fresh water: they can be gritty.

To remove grit from the poaching liquid, strain it too, through either cheesecloth or a very fine strainer.

Boil the poaching liquid briskly. Your aim is to reduce its volume by about one third and consequently intensify its flavor.

As the mushroom stock boils, finely slice the onion, then soften it in a sturdy pan with the oil. Add the rice and toast it with the oil and onion.

Pour the mushroom liquid over the rice and let it cook until the liquid is almost absorbed. If this happens before the rice is cooked – about 15 minutes – add small amounts of water.

When the rice is cooked, stir in the cream and cheese; check the seasoning. Just before serving stir in the mushrooms.

Milanese Risotto

INGREDIENTS *serves 4*

2 tbsp beef marrow
1 small onion, thinly sliced
$^{2}/_{3}$ cup butter
1$^{3}/_{4}$ cup rice
1 cup dry white wine
5 cups beef stock, skimmed of fat
$^{1}/_{8}$ tsp saffron
5 tbsp grated Parmesan cheese

PREPARATION

Scrape the marrow with a knife to remove any bits of bone, then chop and put in a pan with the onion and $^{1}/_{3}$ cup butter. Fry until the onion is soft but not brown. Add the rice and fry for 2 or 3 minutes. Add the wine and cook until absorbed. Add the stock with a ladle, waiting between each addition until it has been absorbed. Cook the rice for 30 minutes.

Ten minutes before the end of cooking time, dissolve the saffron in a few tbsp boiling stock and add to the rice. Finally, add the remaining butter and stir in the Parmesan. Let stand, covered, for 2 minutes before serving.

Country-Style Risotto

INGREDIENTS *serves 4*

vegetable oil
1 onion, chopped
$^{1}/_{2}$ cup shelled fresh peas
$^{1}/_{2}$ cup asparagus tips
$^{3}/_{4}$ cup sliced zucchini
chicken or beef stock
2 cups chopped tomatoes
$^{1}/_{2}$ cup cooked navy beans
salt and pepper
1$^{3}/_{4}$ cups rice
5 tbsp butter
6 tbsp grated Parmesan cheese

PREPARATION

Heat a little oil in a pan, add the onion and cook until soft. Add the peas, asparagus and zucchini and cook for about 5 minutes. Add a little stock and cook over low heat for 10 minutes.

Add the tomatoes and beans; season with salt and pepper. Cook for 15 minutes, then add the rice. Stir and add more stock, as necessary, and cook until *al dente*.

Stir in the butter and 3 tbsp Parmesan. Serve sprinkled with remaining Parmesan.

Artichoke Risotto

INGREDIENTS *serves 4*

4 tbsp butter
1 small onion, finely sliced
1$^{3}/_{4}$ cups Arborio (risotto) rice
2 chicken bouillon cubes *or* 5 cups Pastine in Brodo (see page 56)
2 cans artichoke hearts
4 tbsp double cream
3 tbsp freshly grated Parmesan cheese
salt and pepper to taste

PREPARATION

Melt the butter in a sturdy pan. Soften the onion in it. Add the rice and toast it for 2-3 minutes. (Do not allow either rice or onion to color).

Crumble in the bouillon cube and add 5 cups water. Cook the rice until it is *al dente*. If too much liquid remains in the pan, ladle it out.

As the rice is cooking, drain and wash the artichokes. Gently warm them with the cream and the grated Parmesan. Fold this mixture into the rice as soon as it is cooked. Season and serve immediately.

Saffron

Saffron gives its lovely color to Milan's famous risotto. It comes from the pistils of the autumn-flowering crocus. Half a million pistils are needed to make about 2lb of saffron powder, so it is very expensive.

Above: Milanese risotto

Right: Artichoke risotto

Chef's tips

The dish Artichoke Risotto originates with the baby artichokes – which can be eaten whole, choke and all – in season in Italy during very early spring. If you can find them, use them. Regrettably, they are very rare outside the country.

Sicilian Artichoke Risotto

INGREDIENTS *serves 4*

5 tbsp coarsely chopped bacon
1 onion
1 clove garlic
½ stick celery
1 bunch parsley
vegetable oil
½ cup peeled, seeded, chopped tomato
salt and pepper
1¼ cups artichoke hearts packed in water, drained
2½ cups cold water
1 cup rice
¼ cup grated pecorino cheese

PREPARATION

Chop together the bacon, onion, garlic, celery and parsley and fry in a few tbsp oil. Then add the tomato, season with salt and pepper and cook gently for 10 minutes.

Add the artichoke hearts and cold water and cook for 10 minutes longer. Bring to a boil, add the rice and cook for 20 minutes or until just tender. Stir in the grated pecorino cheese to serve.

Parmesan Risotto

INGREDIENTS *serves 4*
1 small onion
2/3 cup butter
olive oil
5 cups beef stock, skimmed of fat
1 3/4 cups rice
6 tbsp grated Parmesan cheese
salt

PREPARATION
Thinly slice the onion and put in a pan with 4 tbsp butter and 1tbsp oil; cook over low heat until soft but not brown, adding 1 tbsp stock, if necessary. Add the rice and fry for a minute, then add a ladleful of stock. When this has been absorbed, add another and repeat the process until 2 1/2 cups stock is used. Stir in half the remaining butter and 2 tbsp Parmesan. Continue adding stock gradually. When the rice is cooked, season with salt, add the remaining butter and Parmesan and serve.

Rice with Ham and Chicken Livers

INGREDIENTS *serves 4*
1/2 small onion, finely chopped
5 tbsp butter, diced
1/3 cup diced lean pancetta
salt and pepper
1/2 cup dry marsala *or* red wine
1/2 cup sliced chicken livers
1/2 cup julienne-cut prosciutto
1 3/4 cups rice
chicken or beef stock
5 tbsp grated Parmesan cheese

PREPARATION

Fry the onion in 2 tbsp butter, add the pancetta, season with salt and pepper and cook gently for 2 minutes. Add the marsala or red wine and let it evaporate almost completely. Stir in the livers and prosciutto. Add the rice and ladle on stock gradually as rice absorbs it, stirring constantly. Remove the risotto from the heat; stir in remaining butter and a little Parmesan. Leave to stand for 1 minute, then serve sprinkled with remaining Parmesan.

Jumbo Shrimp Risotto

INGREDIENTS *serves 4*

6 tbsp butter
vegetable oil
½ carrot, chopped
½ small onion, chopped
1 stick celery, chopped
about ¼ cup brandy
pinch of dried thyme
⅔ cup dry white wine
1 lb uncooked jumbo shrimp, shelled, deveined, cut into chunks
6 cups chicken stock
1¾ cups rice
salt

PREPARATION

Preheat the oven to 400°F. Heat 3 tbsp butter with 1 tbsp oil in a pan, add the chopped vegetables and cook until they are softened.

Pour in the brandy and add the thyme. Cook gently, stirring, until the liquid has evaporated. Then add the wine and reduce by half. Add the jumbo shrimp and cook for 15 minutes. Keep hot.

Bring the stock to a boil, pour in the rice and add a pinch of salt. Bring back to a boil, then cover and bake for 20 minutes. Drain the rice, fluff with a fork, mix in the remaining butter and pour the jumbo shrimp mixture over it.

Above: Rice with ham and chicken livers *Below: Rice with asparagus*

Rice with Asparagus

INGREDIENTS *serves 4*

1 lb asparagus
vegetable oil
6 tbsp chopped bacon
1 onion, chopped
1 clove garlic, chopped
1 bunch parsley, chopped
salt
1¼ cups rice
½ cup diced caciocavallo cheese

PREPARATION

Clean the asparagus, cut off tough stalk ends and boil for 12 minutes in salted water. Drain, reserving the cooking liquid; cut off asparagus tips.

In a pan, heat the oil and fry the bacon, onion, garlic and parsley. Pour on a little asparagus liquid, season with salt and bring to the boil.

Add the rice, adding more asparagus liquid as it is absorbed. When the rice is cooked, mix in the diced caciocavallo cheese and asparagus tips.

Rice with Lima Beans

INGREDIENTS *serves 4*

3 strips bacon
1 onion
1 clove garlic
½ stick celery
1 bunch parsley
vegetable oil
2 medium tomatoes, peeled, chopped, crushed with a fork
salt and pepper
1½ cups shelled fresh lima beans
1¾ cups rice
grated pecorino cheese

PREPARATION

Chop the bacon, onion, garlic, celery and parsley finely together. Heat a little oil in a pan and cook the mixture gently, stirring.

Add the prepared tomatoes, season with salt and pepper and cook for 10 minutes. Add the lima beans and 6 cups water.

Bring to a boil and add the rice. Cook for 20 minutes or until the rice is done and the consistency is thick and soupy. Sprinkle with pecorino to serve.

Pumpkin Risotto

INGREDIENTS *serves 4*

1lb pumpkin
½ cup butter
4 cups boiling water
1¾ cups rice
2 chicken or beef bouillon cubes
¼ cup grated Parmesan cheese
salt

PREPARATION

Remove the seeds from the pumpkin, then peel and cube. Place the cubed pumpkin and half the butter in a saucepan and fry for a minute, add a ladleful of boiling water and cook gently until half cooked. Add the rice to the pumpkin, stir and fry for a minute; then add a ladleful of boiling water and crumble in bouillon cubes, stirring constantly and adding more water as each ladleful is absorbed. Continue the process until the rice is cooked. Turn off the heat, add the remaining butter and stir in the grated Parmesan cheese. Season with salt to taste and serve.

Mussel Risotto

INGREDIENTS *serves 4*

2lb mussels
vegetable oil
3 cloves garlic, chopped
½ small onion, chopped
6 tbsp butter
1¾ cups rice
salt and pepper
fish stock *or* salted water

PREPARATION

Pull off and discard the beards from the mussels; wash the mussels thoroughly in running water. Put them into a big pan with a little oil and half the garlic and put over a gentle heat. As the mussels open, remove them from their shells and set aside. Strain the cooking liquid and reserve. Soften the remaining garlic and the onion in 4 tbsp butter and a little oil. Add the rice. Season with salt and freshly ground pepper, adding fish stock or salted water a ladleful at a time until the rice is tender. Just before removing from the heat, stir in the mussels and strained mussel liquid; add remaining butter and serve.

R*ice*

Italy is Europe's biggest rice producer. Piedmont and Lombardy are the regions where it is grown. Italian rice has shorter, fatter grains than the Asian variety. It takes a little longer to cook, but has more bite and body and is excellent for risotto and for soups where the grains must remain firm and creamy as well as succulent. Arborio is the variety usually exported. Asian rice is better for timbales, salads and pilafs, because it can be cooked until it is dry and fluffy.

Sardinian Risotto with Tomato Sauce

INGREDIENTS *serves 4*
5 tbsp butter
1¾ cups rice
salt and pepper
2 vegetable bouillon cubes
For the sauce
⅓ cup chopped lean pancetta
vegetable oil
1 clove garlic
½ stick celery
½ small onion
1 small bunch parsley
1 lb tomatoes, chopped
salt and pepper
2 tbsp grated pecorino cheese

PREPARATION
Heat 3 tbsp butter in a pan, add the rice, season with salt and pepper and cook for a few minutes. Pour in 5 cups boiling water and crumble in the bouillon cubes. Stir gently as the rice absorbs the water.

Meanwhile, prepare the sauce. Fry the pancetta in a little oil, remove with a slotted spoon and set aside. Chop the garlic, celery, onion and parsley together, add them to the pancetta drippings and lightly brown. Add the tomatoes, season with salt and pepper and cook for 15 minutes.

Finally, add the pancetta. Remove the rice from the heat, stir in the remaining butter and grated pecorino cheese and pour the hot sauce over.

Above: Sardinian risotto with tomato sauce

Above: Mussel risotto

PIZZA

The pizza originated in Naples, an invention of Neapolitan bakers for the poverty-stricken inhabitants of the back streets of the city, to make a little food stretch a long way. Because it is still a cheap and cheerful way to eat, the pizza has become even more popular in other countries than it is in Italy and there are pizza restaurants all over the world.

Deep Dish Mozzarella and Salami Pizza

INGREDIENTS *makes 2×8in pizzas*

2¼ cups flour made into pizza dough (page 43)
1½ cups canned tomatoes, drained
2 tsp oil
1 tsp oregano
12 slices Italian salami
12 thin slices mozzarella cheese
2 tbsp Parmesan cheese
salt and freshly ground pepper
½ cup black olives

PREPARATION

Make the dough and allow to rise. Punch down and shape in 2×8in pie plates placed on a baking sheet.

Preheat the oven to 425°F. Mash down the tomatoes and add a little of the drained juice. Brush the dough with oil and arrange the tomatoes on the bottom.

Roll the salami into rounds. Sprinkle a little Parmesan cheese on the tomato and then the oregano. Arrange the salami rolls. Place the slices of mozzarella cheese alternately with salami. Season well. Sprinkle on the remaining Parmesan and decorate the whole with black olives.

Brush over with oil and cook in a hot oven for 20 minutes. Reduce the heat to 375°F for a further 5-10 minutes.

Above Pizza fantasia

Page 144: Deep dish mozzarella and salami pizza

Pizza Fantasia

INGREDIENTS *serves 4*

1 recipe pizza dough (page 43)
1¾ cups peeled, chopped tomatoes
finely diced mozzarella cheese
8 flat anchovy fillets, chopped
12 pitted green olives
1 tbsp capers
4 small pickles
marinated artichoke hearts, drained and sliced
pepper
½ cup olive oil

PREPARATION

Preheat the oven to 475°F. Roll out the dough into a circle, put on an oiled baking sheet and cover with tomatoes. Arrange mozzarella, anchovies, olives, capers, pickles and artichokes on top. Sprinkle with pepper and drizzle with oil. Bake for 15 minutes.

Mozzarella

Genuine mozzarella cheeses come from Campania and Apulia and are made with buffalo milk. True mozzarella is increasingly difficult to get hold of because of the scarcity of the buffalo. The cheese commonly available today is made from cow's milk. It should be eaten absolutely fresh and moist and is sold in round balls wrapped in waxed paper to keep it that way. If the cheese has dried out a little, it is best used in cooking or to top pizzas.

Pizza Siciliana

INGREDIENTS *serves 2-4*

2¼ cups flour made into risen pizza dough (page 43)

⅝ cup Tomato Sauce (page 126)

4 tomatoes, skinned and sliced

½ tsp oregano

salt and freshly ground pepper

⅓ cup Parmesan cheese

1 can anchovies

good ½ cup black olives

PREPARATION

Shape the dough into a rectangular shape 12in×8in or use a pie plate or a large jelly roll pan.

Preheat the oven to 425°F. Paint the dough with a pastry brush dipped in oil and then cover the surface with the tomato sauce. Place the sliced tomatoes on top and sprinkle with oregano and seasoning. Sprinkle with Parmesan cheese.

Drain the can of anchovies and arrange the halved fillets in a lattice design. Place an olive in the center of each lattice.

Paint over with the remaining oil and bake in a hot oven for 15 minutes. Then turn the heat down to 375°F for a further 10 minutes.

Family Pizza

INGREDIENTS *serves 4*

2¾ cups flour made into risen pizza dough (page 43)

⅝ cup Tomato Sauce I (page 126)

1 can chopped tomatoes

1 green pepper

½ tsp oregano

salt and freshly ground black pepper

¾ cup grated Cheddar cheese

3 pork sausages

PREPARATION

Make the pizza up as the Siciliana as far as painting the dough with the oil and arranging the sauce on top. Add the chopped tomatoes. Dice the green bell pepper into small pieces, blanch it for 20 minutes and drain it. Scatter the oregano and pepper on the tomato mixture, followed by the grated Cheddar. Cut the pork sausages in pieces diagonally and arrange on the top of the pizza. Cook as for Pizza Siciliana.

Below: Pizza Siciliana

Deep Dish Mushroom and Prosciutto Pizza

INGREDIENTS *makes 2 8in pizzas*

2¼ cups wholewheat flour made into risen pizza dough (page 43)

Topping

1 tbsp oil
1½ cups canned tomatoes, drained
4 tomatoes, skinned and sliced
1 tsp oregano
2 tbsp Parmesan cheese
12oz mushrooms, washed and sliced
8 slices thin prosciutto
salt and freshly ground pepper

PREPARATION

Shape the dough in 2×8in pie plates placed on a baking sheet. Paint the shaped dough with a pastry brush dipped in oil.

Preheat the oven to 425°F. Arrange the tomatoes on the bases of the pizza dough. Sprinkle with oregano and salt and pepper. Sprinkle half the cheese over the tomato mixture.

Melt the butter and the remaining oil in a skillet and allow the mushrooms to cook over a low heat for about 4 minutes.

Spread the mushrooms on top of the pizzas and arrange the ham on top. Sprinkle with the remaining cheese.

Cook in a hot oven for 15 minutes, before turning the oven down to 375°F for the last 10 minutes.

Left: Deep dish mushroom and prosciutto pizza

Wholewheat Pepper and Caper Pizza

INGREDIENTS *Makes 2 8in pizzas*

2¼ cups wholewheat flour made into risen pizza dough (page 43)

Topping

1 tbsp oil
1½ cups canned tomatoes
½ tsp fresh or ¼ tsp dried thyme
6oz mushrooms, washed and sliced
1 red pepper, seeded
1 tbsp capers, chopped
salt and freshly ground pepper
2 tbsp Parmesan cheese

PREPARATION

Shape the dough in 2×8in pie plates placed on a baking sheet and brush with oil.

Preheat the oven to 425°F. Drain and chop the tomatoes, mix with the thyme and spread on the pizza bases. Arrange the mushrooms on the two bases and sprinkle with chopped capers. Season well with salt and pepper.

Sprinkle with grated cheese and arrange strips of red pepper on top. Bake for 15 minutes in a hot oven and then reduce the temperature to 375°F for another 10 minutes.

Wholewheat Eggplant *and* Mozzarella Pizza

INGREDIENTS *makes one 8in pizza*

1 cup wholewheat flour made into risen pizza dough (see page 43)
2 tbsp oil
1 small eggplant, sliced
salt and freshly ground pepper
$^{5}/_{8}$ cup Tomato Sauce I (see page 126)
1 small red pepper, seeded
3 stuffed olives, halved
2oz sliced mozzarella cheese

PREPARATION

Shape the pizza into a 8in round and rub a little oil over the dough.

Preheat the oven to 425°F. Sprinkle the sliced eggplant with salt and allow it to stand for a few minutes. Spread the tomato sauce over the dough. Cut six rings of red pepper.

Heat the remaining oil in the skillet. Drain the eggplant slices of juice on paper towels and fry for about 30 seconds on each side.

Arrange them on the pizza with a ring of red pepper on top and half an olive in the center. Place the slices of mozzarella between the eggplant slices and cook in a hot oven for 15 minutes. Turn the heat down to 375°F for the final 10 minutes of cooking.

Individual Pizzas *with* Anchovies

INGREDIENTS *serves 4*

2lb fresh anchovies
$2^{1}/_{4}$ cups flour made into risen pizza dough (see page 43)
pepper and salt
2 cloves garlic, crushed
2 tbsp chopped parsley
olive oil

PREPARATION

Preheat the oven to 475°C. Remove the heads from the anchovies, wash and dry well. (Use canned anchovies if fresh ones are not available.)

Roll the dough into four thin circles and put on a greased baking sheet. Arrange the anchovies on the pizzas and season with pepper and a little salt. Sprinkle the anchovies with garlic and parsley and moisten with a few spoonfuls of oil. Bake for 30 minutes and serve at once.

Deep Dish Artichoke Heart *and* Bacon Pizza

INGREDIENTS *makes 2 8in pizzas*

$2^{1}/_{4}$ cups flour made into risen pizza dough (see page 43).
1tbsp olive oil
$1^{1}/_{4}$ cups Tomato Sauce II (see page 126)
1 can artichoke hearts
12 slices bacon
1tbsp Parmesan cheese
1tbsp freshly chopped basil or parsley leaves

PREPARATION

Shape the risen dough into 2×8in pie plates or sandwich cake pans.

Preheat the oven to 425°F. Brush over the dough with the oil and divide the tomato sauce between the two bases. Drain the artichoke hearts. Roll up the slices of bacon and cook under the broiler or in the oven for a few minutes.

Sprinkle the pizzas with Parmesan cheese and herbs. Arrange the artichoke hearts alternately with the bacon rolls. Brush over with the remaining oil.

Cook in a hot oven for 15-20 minutes before reducing the heat to 375°F for a further 5 minutes.

Right: Deep dish artichoke heart and bacon pizza

Neapolitan Pizza

INGREDIENTS *makes one 12in pizza*

2¼ cups flour made into risen pizza dough (see page 43)
1 tbsp olive oil
1 clove garlic, crushed
6 tomatoes, skinned and sliced
½ tsp oregano
4 chopped basil leaves

PREPARATION

Preheat the oven to 425°F. Take the dough and roll into a round shape, kneading the round out to 12in size with floured knuckles. Make sure that it is not too thick. Any left-over dough can be allowed to rise and cooked as a bread roll.

A large pie plate is ideal for this type of pizza but it shapes well on a greased baking tray.

Brush over the dough with the olive oil and rub over the whole surface with the well crushed clove of garlic.

Arrange the tomatoes over the surface and sprinkle with herbs. Fresh parsley may be used if basil is unobtainable. Season well. Place in a hot oven for 20-25 minutes.

This is the basic tomato pizza but most people prefer to add extra ingredients.

Left: Neapolitan pizza

Deep Dish Ham and Mushroom Pizza

INGREDIENTS *makes 2×8in pizzas*

2¼ cups flour made into risen pizza dough (page 43)
1 tbsp oil
1¼ cups well flavored Béchamel Sauce (page 122)
salt and freshly ground pepper
1½ cups canned tomatoes, drained
½ tsp oregano
6 slices cooked ham
4oz mushrooms, washed and sliced
4oz mozzarella cheese, thinly sliced

PREPARATION

Shape the risen dough into 2×8in pie plates. Preheat the oven to 425°F.

Brush over the dough with oil and divide the Béchamel sauce between the two bases. Arrange half the sliced mushrooms on the Béchamel sauce. Chop the canned tomatoes and divide between the two bases. Season well and sprinkle with oregano.

Cut the slices of ham in two and roll them up, placing six rolls on each pizza, alternating with thin slices of mozzarella cheese. Garnish with sliced mushrooms.

Bake in a hot oven for 15 minutes and then reduce the heat to 375°F for a further 10 minutes.

These pizzas make a very substantial meal; just two of them should serve four average appetites.

Pizza Toppings

Topping for pizza marinara
3 medium firm-ripe tomatoes (not watery)
2-3 cloves garlic
dried oregano
olive oil
coarse salt

Topping for pizza 4 stagioni
cooked clams
cooked mussels
pitted ripe olives cut into pieces
flat anchovy fillets
marinated artichoke hearts

Topping for pizza Margherita
thin slivers of mozzarella cheese
tomatoes
shredded fresh basil
grated pecorino cheese
salt
olive oil

Other suggested toppings:
capers
chopped pitted ripe olives
chopped pitted green olives
marinated mushrooms
roasted peppers cut into strips
seafood (add near the end of cooking time)
flaked tuna
sliced cooked ham
cubed salami
sliced pancetta
sliced sausage
cubed Fontina cheese
Gruyère, Gorgonzola, Gouda cheeses (grated or sliced)
sliced hard-boiled eggs
fresh or dried basil, marjoram, parsley

VEGETABLES

Fresh vegetables are the delight of the Italian market place. Fennel, baby peas, artichokes, asparagus, lima beans, chestnuts, mushrooms, eggplants, peppers, zucchini and tomatoes are all eaten in their proper seasons, and often make a complete course in themselves.

Fennel Milanese Style

INGREDIENTS *serves 4-6*
3 medium fennel bulbs
⅔ cup white wine
2tbsp vinegar
1 clove garlic
2 bay leaves
salt to taste
2 eggs
3 cups fresh breadcrumbs
⅔ cup olive oil

PREPARATION
The fennel, though bulb-like, is also slightly flattened. So cut it into ¼in slices from the root upwards, in the same plane as its flat side. You will find that the inner three or four slices hang together as cross-sections of the plant. Set all these aside.

Put the rest, with the white wine, vinegar, garlic and bay leaves, into 3¾ cups water, and bring everything to a boil. Salt the liquid to taste and poach the fennel cross sections in it for 10-15 minutes or until soft. Drain the fennel and pat it dry.

In a shallow bowl, beat the two eggs well. Dip each fennel piece into the egg, covering it well. Shake off any excess. Now press the fennel slices forcefully into the breadcrumbs, spread out on an open surface to facilitate the process.

Heat the oil to a fast-frying temperature; fry each fennel slice until crisp on both sides. Eat while hot.

Page 154: Fennel Milanese style

Cabbage with Bacon and Potatoes

INGREDIENTS *serves 6*
1 (about 2lb) head leafy cabbage
about ¾ cup butter
¾ cup chopped smoked pancetta
chicken stock
salt and pepper
ground nutmeg
1¼lb potatoes
milk
2 egg yolks

PREPARATION
Preheat the oven to 350°F. Trim the cabbage and blanch in salted water for 10 minutes. Drain and squeeze out the water, then chop coarsely.

Heat a little butter in a large pan, add the pancetta and cabbage, stir well and cover with stock. Season with salt, pepper and nutmeg and bring to a boil, then simmer over medium heat for 45 minutes.

Boil the potatoes in another pan. Peel, then press through a strainer or mash well while still hot. Put the mashed potatoes in a small saucepan over medium heat, add 4 tbsp butter and enough milk to give a soft, but not runny, consistency. Season and mix in the egg yolks.

Butter the baking dish, spoon in the cabbage mixture and pipe on mashed potatoes. Dot the top with the remaining butter and bake for 10 minutes. Serve hot.

Chef's tips

You can make soup with the spinach stalks, as you can with the juices of the spinach, if you go to the trouble of keeping it for later use, either in the refrigerator or in the freezer.

Fried Radicchio

INGREDIENTS *serves 4*
8 heads radicchio
virgin olive oil
salt and pepper

PREPARATION
Wash the radicchio well without removing the leaves and drain off as much water as possible. Then cut into quarters from stem to tip and squeeze out more excess water (otherwise the oil will spit when heated). Put them on a plate and sprinkle with oil, salt and freshly ground pepper. Put a large skillet on to heat and, when hot, put in radicchio and cook briskly, turning over as soon as each side is cooked. Arrange on a serving dish. This method results in crisp radicchio – for softer radicchio, cook, covered, over lower heat.

Spinach with Oil, Lemon and Pepper

INGREDIENTS *serves 4-6*
2lb fresh spinach
⅔ cup olive oil
juice of half a lemon
salt and a copious quantity of freshly ground black pepper

PREPARATION
Trim the stalks from the spinach leaves (see Chef's Tips).

Very lightly oil the bottom of a thick pan and set in on a low heat. Introduce the spinach a little at a time. It will shrink as it comes in contact with the heat. Cover the pan and steam the spinach for about 10 minutes over a fairly low heat.

When the spinach is cooked, press it lightly in a colander and secure the juices for another use (see Chef's Tips). Allow the spinach to cool slightly. Then simply dress it with the olive oil, lemon juice, salt and black pepper.

Eat it hot, warm or cool.

Above: Spinach with oil, lemon and pepper

Right: Cabbage with bacon and potatoes

Asparagus with Eggs and Cheese

INGREDIENTS *serves 4*
3lb asparagus
4 eggs
6 tbsp butter
3 tbsp grated Parmesan cheese

PREPARATION
Clean the asparagus and cut off tough stalk ends; boil or steam asparagus. Drain and arrange on a heated serving dish. Fry the eggs in about 4 tbsp butter just until set. Heat the remaining butter separately. Sprinkle the Parmesan on the asparagus, put the just-set eggs carefully on top, then drizzle with melted butter. Serve at once while piping hot.

Chef's aside

The simplest is the best. Cooked in this way, the eggplants steam in their own juices, hermetically sealed by their skins. The flavored steam also picks up the scent of the garlic and forces it through the plant. Magnificent.

Baked Aubergines (Eggplants) with Mozzarella

INGREDIENTS *serves 4*
2 medium eggplants
4tbsp olive oil
1lb fresh or canned plum tomatoes
2 tbsp fresh oregano (half the quantity for dried)
salt and freshly ground black pepper
225g/8oz mozzarella cheese
3 tbsp freshly grated Parmesan cheese

PREPARATION
Preheat the oven to 400°F. Cut off the coarse stalks of the eggplants and slice them lengthways in ½in slices. Bake the slices in the oven, directly on the wire shelving, for 10 minutes or until very soft.

In the meantime, oil a baking dish. Chop the tomatoes roughly and combine with the oregano. Season strongly with the salt and pepper. Grate the mozzarella and mix it with the Parmesan.

Remove the eggplant slices from the oven and line the baking dish with one layer. Spread the tomato and oregano mixture evenly over it, and sprinkle the mozzarella and Parmesan on top of that. Continue these layers until the dish is full, leaving yourself a good amount of mozzarella and Parmesan as a final, thick coating: the cheese will melt and seal the dish as it cooks.

Bake until the cheese melts and browns – about 15-20 minutes.

Eggplant Baked with Garlic Sott'olio

INGREDIENTS *serves 4-6*
2 large eggplants
4 cloves garlic
⅔ cup olive oil
juice of half a lemon
salt and freshly ground black pepper

PREPARATION
Preheat the oven to 400°F. Cut the spiky stalk off the eggplants. Peel the garlic cloves and cut them lengthways into thinnish slivers.

Pierce the eggplants all over with a thin-bladed knife. Push the slivers of garlic into the slits.

Place the eggplants directly onto the wire shelving of the oven. Do *not* oil them in any way. Bake for 15 minutes, until the vegetables shrink into themselves and the skins wrinkle. When cooked, they will feel soft to the touch.

Remove the eggplants from the oven and allow them to stand for 3-4 minutes.

Slice them into neat, thin, strips lengthways. Dress them with the oil, lemon juice, salt and pepper. Serve the eggplants hot, warm or cool.

Right: Eggplant baked with garlic sott'olio

Leafy Cabbage Stuffed with Scamorza Cheese

INGREDIENTS *serves 4*

1lb head leafy cabbage
6oz thinly sliced scamorza or mozzarella cheese
vegetable oil
1tbsp chopped onion
1¼lb tomatoes, peeled, seeded, pressed through a strainer
salt and pepper
few tbsp grated Parmesan cheese

PREPARATION

Preheat the oven to 350°F. Trim the cabbage stem and remove the outer leaves. Boil or steam the whole cabbage until cooked but still firm. Allow to cool.

Remove the leaves and divide into 8 piles. Fill the top leaf in each pile with scamorza or mozzarella and roll up each pile around the cheese. Heat a little oil in a skillet and fry onion until soft. Add the tomatoes, season with salt and pepper and cook over medium heat until very soft, being careful not to let the sauce dry out.

Put a layer of tomato sauce in a baking dish, arrange cabbage rolls on top and pour the remaining sauce over. Sprinkle with Parmesan, bake for 10 minutes and serve while piping hot.

Country-Style Zucchini

INGREDIENTS *serves 4*

1lb zucchini
1 egg
salt
⅓ cup breadcrumbs
butter
vegetable oil
1 onion, sliced
1lb tomatoes, peeled, seeded, chopped
1½ tsp sugar
pepper
½ cup grated Parmesan cheese
1tbsp chopped fresh basil
4 fresh mint leaves, chopped

PREPARATION

Preheat the oven to 350°F. Cut the ends off the zucchini and cut lengthways. Beat the egg with a little salt. Dip the zucchini in egg, and then in breadcrumbs. Melt a little butter in a pan with some oil and fry the zucchini until golden. Drain on paper towels. Set aside.

Heat ¼ cup oil in a pan and cook the onion for 5 minutes. Add the tomatoes, sugar, salt and pepper, cover and cook over medium heat for 30 minutes, stirring occasionally.

Butter a baking dish, put in a layer of zucchini, cover with a little tomato sauce, sprinkle with Parmesan, basil and mint, and continue the layers like this until all the ingredients have been used up. End with sauce and bake for 15 minutes.

This dish can be served hot but is also delicious lukewarm or cold.

Below: Leafy cabbage stuffed with scamorza cheese

Country-Style Peppers and Tomatoes

INGREDIENTS *serves 4*
¼ cup butter
vegetable oil
1lb green onions
4 large green or yellow peppers, seeded, cut into strips
1lb tomatoes, peeled, seeded, chopped
salt
4 hard-boiled eggs, chopped

PREPARATION
Heat the butter with some oil in a pan and fry the green onions and peppers until half cooked. (If desired, you may roast and peel the peppers before sautéeing with the onions.) Then add the tomatoes, season with salt, add a little lukewarm water and cook over medium heat, stirring occasionally. As soon as the peppers are cooked, stir in the eggs and serve.

Above: Country-style peppers and tomatoes

Artichoke Hearts with Spinach

INGREDIENTS *serves 4*
8 artichoke hearts
juice of 1 lemon
olive oil
all-purpose flour
1¼lb fresh spinach
3 tbsp butter
salt and pepper
1 tbsp grated Parmesan cheese

For the sauce
¼ cup butter
2 tbsp all-purpose flour
⅔ cup milk
⅔ cup whipping cream
salt and pepper
ground nutmeg
¼ cup shredded Swiss cheese

To assemble
2 tbsp grated Parmesan cheese
3 tbsp breadcrumbs
1 tbsp butter

PREPARATION
Preheat the oven to 375°F. Steam or boil the artichoke hearts in water acidulated with lemon juice, to which you have added 1tbsp oil and 1tsp flour.

Meanwhile trim and wash the spinach in several changes of water, then boil in the water clinging to the leaves. When cooked, rinse in cold water and squeeze dry.

Melt 3 tbsp butter in a pan, add the spinach, season with salt and pepper and cook over a low heat until butter is absorbed. Then stir in 1tbsp Parmesan.

For the sauce, melt ¼ cup butter in a small pan and add the flour, blending well with a wooden spoon to avoid lumps forming. Add the milk and cream, season with salt, pepper and nutmeg and cook, stirring, until the sauce has thickened and is simmering. Stir in the cheese and remove from heat.

To assemble, grease a large baking dish. Cut a thin slice off the bottom of the artichoke hearts so that they stand upright and arrange them in a dish. Divide the spinach between them, molding equally on top, pour over the sauce, sprinkle with 2 tbsp Parmesan and breadcrumbs and dot with 1 tbsp butter. Bake for 10 minutes or until golden. Serve at once.

Broccoli with Green Pepper and Garlic

INGREDIENTS *serves 4-6*

1½lb fresh broccoli cut into flowerets
salt to taste
2 tbsp olive oil
1 small green pepper, deseeded and finely sliced
4 cloves garlic
¾ tbsp freshly grated Parmesan cheese
freshly ground black pepper

PREPARATION

Bring plenty of salted water to a boil. Drop in the trimmed broccoli flowerets and boil for 3 minutes. Drain them and stop the cooking process by plunging them immediately into cold water.

Heat the olive oil over a high flame. Cook the pepper in the oil until the slices begin to brown slightly at the edges. Reduce the heat to a simmer and add the garlic cloves, well crushed. Cook the pepper and garlic together for 1-2 minutes.

Add the broccoli and the grated Parmesan cheese, turn in the oil and Parmesan until the broccoli is hot.

Serve immediately, lavishly sprinkled with the pepper.

Chef's tip

The Parmesan is as much for grain as for taste – hence the small quantity.

Artichokes

The artichoke is an edible thistle and has had a place of honor in kitchen gardens since the Renaissance. The Italians have a huge variety of artichoke recipes, including some for young artichokes eaten whole.

Soak artichokes upside down in a bowl of cold water acidulated with vinegar or lemon juice. Cut off the stem near the base of the vegetable and cut the tips cleanly off the leaves. Rub any cut edges with lemon juice.

Bring a large pan of salted, acidulated water to a boil. Put the artichokes in, stem down, bring back to a boil and test after 30 minutes to see if they are done. Tug at a leaf at the base of the largest artichoke – if it comes away easily, the artichokes are done. Drain them upside down in a colander.

To eat, pull away the leaves, beginning at the base. Dip the succulent base of the leaf in the sauce provided and nibble away the fleshy part. When all the leaves have been removed, discard the choke. Eat the delicious heart of the artichoke with a knife and fork and more of the sauce. To prepare artichokes for stuffing, slice off the top as well as the stem before you boil it. When it is cooked, remove the inner leaves and the choke so that you are left with a cup.

If only the heart is needed, cook the artichokes in the usual way. Dismantle each artichoke, as if you were eating if, to uncover the heart.

Gratinéed Jerusalem Artichokes

INGREDIENTS *serves 4-6*

1lb Jerusalem artichokes (see Chef's Tips)
salt
4 tbsp butter
3 tbsp freshly grated Parmesan cheese
freshly grated black pepper

PREPARATION

Preheat the oven to 400°F. Scrub the artichokes in a robust fashion and cut away any darker patches of skin. (There is no need to peel them.)

Drop the artichokes in boiling salted water – cover well – and cook for 10 minutes. They should be firm but easily biteable. Remove them from their cauldron, drain and slice thinly.

Grease a baking dish with a little of the butter and layer it with the artichokes. Dot the rest of the butter over the top.

Sprinkle with the parmesan and a stiff measure of pepper. Bake them until the cheese and butter form an enticing brown crust. Serve very hot.

Chef's tips

These artichokes are, as you probably know, nothing to do with the other sort. They resemble heavily mis-shapen potatoes or fresh root ginger. Their unique and delectable flavor makes splendid soups, especially when puréed with chicken stock.

Right: Broccoli with green pepper and garlic

Above: Zucchini fried in light batter

Beets with Cream and Mushrooms

INGREDIENTS *serves 4*
5 tbsp butter
vegetable oil
1½ cups sliced fresh mushrooms
1 clove garlic, chopped
3lb beets, cooked, peeled, chopped
2 eggs
3 tbsp whipping cream
1½ tbsp grated Parmesan cheese
salt and pepper
breadcrumbs

PREPARATION

Preheat the oven to 350°F. Melt the butter with a little oil in a skillet, add the mushrooms and garlic and fry until soft. Stir in the beets and cook gently so that the flavors mingle. Put the eggs in a bowl with the cream and Parmesan and beat together well. Season with salt and pepper. Add the beet mixture and stir well to coat in egg mixture. Grease a baking dish, sprinkle with breadcrumbs and fill with beet mixture, levelling off the top. Sprinkle with breadcrumbs again, drizzle a little oil over the top and bake until golden.

Leeks in Béchamel Sauce

INGREDIENTS *serves 4*
1¼lb leeks
2 tbsp butter
⅓ cup julienne-cut cooked ham
1 cup Béchamel Sauce with 1 egg yolk added
¼ cup grated Gruyère cheese

PREPARATION

Preheat the oven to 400°F. Trim the leeks, discarding the green tops, and wash well. Boil in lightly salted water, drain and arrange in a baking dish. Dot with butter, cover with ham and pour Béchamel Sauce over the top. Sprinkle with Gruyère and bake until golden brown.

Zucchini Fried in Light Batter

INGREDIENTS *serves 4*
1lb zucchini
1 cup all-purpose flour
salt and pepper to taste
1¼ cups vegetable oil

PREPARATION

Slice the zucchini into batons approximately ½in thick and 2in long, depending on the size of the individual vegetables.

Sift the all-purpose flour with the salt and pepper, then mix it very gradually with water, beating the mixture constantly to avoid lumps forming. Stop adding water when your batter reaches the consistency of thick cream.

Heat the oil until very hot, dip the zucchini in the batter, and then fry them in batches – they should fit only loosely into the pan so that they brown evenly. When the batter is crisp and brown, the vegetables are ready.

Like all fried food, these zucchini should be served very hot.

Chef's tip

It is sometimes difficult to recommend quantities of oil in cases like this. Since this recipe requires deep frying, the depth, with a fixed volume of oil, will clearly vary with the diameter of the pan. Bear in mind that there should be enough oil for the sliced zucchini to float.

Spinach Roman *Style*

INGREDIENTS *serves 4*
2lb fresh spinach
vegetable oil
1 clove garlic, crushed
1/3 cup finely diced bacon
3 tbsp pine nuts
3 tbsp golden raisins, soaked in lukewarm water until plump
salt
butter

PREPARATION
Wash the spinach, discarding tough stalks and discolored leaves. Cook gently in the water clinging to leaves, then drain and squeeze dry. Heat a little oil in a pan, add garlic, bacon and spinach, and cook, gently stirring. After a few minutes, add the pine nuts and golden raisins. Remove from the heat, season with salt, put in a serving dish, top with about 1tbsp butter and serve.

Mushrooms Fried *with* Garlic *and* Parsley

INGREDIENTS *serves 6*
1½lb good mushrooms (see Chef's Tips)
¼ cup olive oil
3 cloves garlic, crushed
2 heaping tbsp chopped fresh parsley
salt and freshly ground black pepper to taste

PREPARATION
Wash but do not peel – *never* peel – the mushrooms. Slice or chop them into thumb-sized chunks if they are particularly large.

Heat the oil to medium and sauté the crushed garlic for 30 seconds or so. Add the mushrooms. These will absorb the oil very promptly. When they do, turn down the heat and wait for the process to reverse – the mushrooms begin to give off their own liquor. This will take 2 minutes or so.

Increase the heat and add the parsley, salt and pepper. Cook on for a further 2-3 minutes and serve.

Chef's tips

The Italian verb "to fry with garlic and parsley" is *trifolare* and you will find quite a number of things *trifolati* – zucchini for example. And what is a good mushroom? What is *not* a good mushroom is that small, white, perfectly symmetrical item that looks like a children's storybook illustration.

Below: Mushrooms fried with garlic and parsley

FISH

Because the Italians are firm believers in using only fresh local produce, you will be unlikely to find seafood in Italy at any distance from the coast. Fish — whether from sea or rivers — is perhaps at its best simply cooked with butter or olive oil, a few leaves of sage and served with a wedge of lemon.

Trout al Carpione

INGREDIENTS *serves 6*

6 medium rainbow trout
1 egg
1¼ cups olive oil
1 cup all-purpose flour
1 large onion
4 cloves of garlic
⅔ cup dry white wine
2 tbsp vinegar
2 tbsp sugar
2 large sprigs rosemary
4 fresh bay leaves
1 chili pepper
salt to taste

PREPARATION

Clean and dry the fish. Beat the egg and mix with its own volume of water.

Heat about one third of the oil to a medium heat, dip the whole fish in the egg/water mixture and then roll in the flour. Fry gently until cooked – whole trout will take 8 minutes per side. When cooking fish in this way *always turn it once only.*

Carefully remove the fish when it is cooked and arrange it attractively on a serving dish.

Set the rest of the olive oil on a medium heat. Slice the onion very finely and stew it in the oil. (Stew, not fry!) Add the garlic and cook both together until the onion is completely soft. Neither must brown.

Add the wine, vinegar, sugar, rosemary, bay leaves and the whole chili. Bring everything to a boil and season. Pour the mixture over the fish and serve either warm, cool or chilled.

Above: Fried stuffed sardines

Page 166: Trout al carpione

Fried Stuffed Sardines

INGREDIENTS *serves 4*

16 fresh sardines
olive oil
2 tbsp dried mushrooms, soaked, drained
1 tbsp fresh breadcrumbs, softened in a little milk and squeezed dry
1 tbsp grated Parmesan cheese
1 clove garlic, crushed
1 tsp chopped fresh marjoram
pinch of dried oregano
4 eggs
salt and pepper
all-purpose flour
fine dry breadcrumbs

PREPARATION

Clean the sardines, removing the heads and tails. Open them out, remove the bones, wash and pat dry. Heat a little olive oil in a skillet, chop the mushrooms finely and fry gently for a few minutes. Transfer them to a dish and add fresh breadcrumbs, Parmesan, garlic, marjoram, oregano, two eggs and a pinch of salt.

Stuff the sardines with this mixture, then close them up. Beat the remaining two eggs with salt and pepper. Dip the stuffed sardines first into flour, then into seasoned beaten egg, then into dry breadcrumbs. Fry in hot oil and serve immediately.

Brochettes of Monkfish with Basil and Orange

INGREDIENTS *serves 4*

2lb monkfish
2 oranges
$^2/_3$ cup olive oil
1 tbsp finely chopped fresh basil
$^1/_2$ cup fresh breadcrumbs
salt and freshly grated black pepper

PREPARATION

Skin the monkfish and dice it into 2in square chunks.

Squeeze the juice from the oranges. Cut the rinds into chunks about the size of the monkfish pieces and reserve. Combine the olive oil, the orange juice and the basil.

Add the fish to the marinade and scatter with the pieces of orange rind. Marinade for up to 2 hours.

Preheat the broiler to its maximum heat. Thread the fish on to skewers, alternating the pieces whenever you can with pieces of orange rind.

Brush liberally with the marinade once more. Sprinkle the side you are broiling first with half the breadcrumbs. Broil for 6-7 minutes. Turn, breadcrumb the other side, and broil again. Remove the brochettes to a serving platter.

Combine any pan juices with what remains of the marinade. Bring to a rapid boil, season and pour over the fish.

Fried Squid

INGREDIENTS *serves 6*

$4^1/_2$lb small squid
$1^1/_2$ cups all-purpose flour
salt and freshly ground black pepper
$2^1/_2$ cups vegetable oil
3 lemons

PREPARATION

Clean the squid (see Chef's Tips on page 94). Slice the body sacs into rings – 5 or 6 per body for small animals.

Heat the oil until it is almost smoking. Here you must use your imagination a little. You are going to fry the squid in batches small enough not to produce a serious drop in the oil temperature. If in any doubt, start with just 2 or 3 and slowly work up.

Dip the squid in the flour, one batch at a time so the coating does not become soggy, shake off the excess and fry until light brown – about 30-40 seconds if the temperature is right. Set each batch to drain on paper towels.

Check for salt once more when all is cooked and serve very hot, with the lemon cut into wedges.

Below: Fried squid

Skate with Anchovy Butter

INGREDIENTS *serves 4*
2lb skate
2 small carrots, chopped
1 stick celery, chopped
2 small onions, chopped
5 tbsp butter
¼ cup all-purpose flour
salt and pepper
1tbsp capers
1tbsp sliced dill pickle
1tbsp chopped parsley
squeeze of lemon juice
5 flat anchovy fillets soaked in milk

PREPARATION
Poach the skate in a court bouillon made from 3 cups water, the carrots, celery and onions. When the fish is cooked, transfer to a serving platter and keep warm.

Melt 2½ tbsp butter, blend in the flour and a little fish poaching liquid. Season with salt and pepper and simmer, stirring, for 7-8 minutes until the sauce has thickened and is smooth and velvety. Add the capers, sliced dill pickle, parsley and lemon juice.

Drain the anchovies and pound with the remaining butter. Blend the anchovy butter into the sauce. Heat through, pour over the skate and serve.

Above: Dried cod Sicilian style

Dried Cod Sicilian Style

INGREDIENTS *serves 4*
1¾lb dried cod, already soaked
olive oil
1 small onion, chopped
1 large clove garlic, chopped
½ cup white wine
1¼lb tomatoes, peeled, seeded, pressed through a strainer
salt and pepper
¾ cup pitted ripe olives
1½ tbsp capers
1 tbsp golden raisins, soaked in lukewarm water until plump
1tbsp pine nuts
3 medium potatoes, peeled, sliced

PREPARATION
Preheat the oven to 375°F. Remove the bones and skin from the cod and cut the flesh into cubes. Heat some oil in an ovenproof saucepan, fry the onion and garlic and add the fish. Cook for a minute, then add the wine.

When the wine has almost evaporated, add the tomatoes and enough water to cover the fish. Season with salt and freshly ground pepper. Bring to a boil, cover and bake for an hour. Add the olives, capers, golden raisins, pine nuts and potatoes. Continue to bake until the potatoes are done and serve immediately.

Braised Swordfish with Peppers

INGREDIENTS *serves 4*

4 swordfish steaks (about 6oz each)
4tbsp olive oil
4 cloves garlic
1 medium onion, roughly chopped
1 medium red bell pepper
¼lb fresh or canned plum tomatoes, roughly chopped
1 chili pepper
⅔ cup dry white wine
salt and pepper to taste

PREPARATION

Wash and thoroughly dry the steaks. Heat the oil over a high heat and seal each steak on each side.

Remove the fish from the pan and reserve it. Turn down the heat to medium and add the whole cloves of garlic and the onions.

Turn the heat once more to high and cook the onions until the edges begin to catch. Reduce the flame to a gentle simmer and cook on until the onions and garlic are softened. In the meantime, de-seed and finely slice the peppers.

When the onions are soft, add the peppers and cook until they begin to soften – about 5 minutes. Add the tomatoes, the whole chili and the wine. Bring to a fierce boil, then add the fish. Turn the heat to a low simmer and cover the pan. Simmer until the fish is very tender – about 15 minutes.

Remove the fish from the pan and set it aside in a warm place. Boil up the pan juices very briskly, until they are reduced to a thick, creamy mixture. Season, pour around the fish and serve.

Baked Stuffed Sardines

INGREDIENTS *serves 4*

16 fresh sardines
2 tbsp vinegar
salt and pepper
⅔ cup mixed chopped garlic, chopped parsley and grated Parmesan cheese
all-purpose flour
2 eggs, beaten
breadcrumbs
olive oil
lemon wedges

PREPARATION

Preheat the oven to 375°F. Clean the sardines, removing the heads and tails, open them out and remove the bones. Wash and pat dry. Arrange on a big dish, sprinkle with vinegar, salt and pepper and stuff each one with the garlic, parsley and cheese mixture.

Close the fish up again, pressing down well; dip them first in flour, then in beaten egg and then in breadcrumbs. Put the sardines in a greased baking dish, sprinkle with oil and bake for 25-30 minutes. Serve with lemon wedges.

Below: Braised swordfish with peppers

Small Salmon with Aïoli

INGREDIENTS *serves 4*
2lb salmon
2 small carrots, chopped
1 stick celery, chopped
2 small onions, chopped
1 tbsp chopped parsley
3 medium potatoes, peeled and sliced
4 cloves garlic
2 slices white bread, crusts trimmed, softened in vinegar
salt and pepper
1 cup vegetable oil
lemon wedges
¼ cup butter, melted

PREPARATION
Clean and wash the salmon, put in a fish kettle or a pan that it will fit and cover with a court bouillon made from 6 cups water, the carrots, celery, onions and parsley. Bring to a gentle boil and simmer for 12 minutes or until the fish is done. Boil the potatoes in salted water.

In a mortar, pound the garlic with the bread, season with salt and pepper and gradually add oil, as if you were making mayonnaise. Drain the salmon, put on to a dish and surround with lemon wedges. Drain the boiled potatoes, drizzle with melted butter, and serve with the fish; pass the aïoli separately.

Salad of Fresh Tuna and Bacon from the Broiler

INGREDIENTS *serves 4*
2lb fresh tuna
1lb bacon *or* pancetta
4 tbsp fresh oregano
⅔ cup olive oil
juice of 1 lemon
2 cloves garlic, well crushed
salt and freshly ground black pepper to taste
1½ tbsp freshly grated Parmesan cheese

PREPARATION
Dice the tuna into thumb-size chunks. Lay the bacon out in flat strips and spread it with the oregano, very finely chopped.

Lay a piece of tuna at the start of each bacon strip, roll in the bacon and pin with a toothpick. Continue thus down each strip of bacon until all the tuna is wrapped.

Combine the olive oil and lemon juice and add the garlic. Marinade the pinned pieces of tuna and bacon in the mixture for about 2 hours.

Preheat the broiler to its highest setting. Thread the bacon and fish chunks on to skewers. Imagine the skewers have four faces. Broil each face for 2 minutes – a quarter turn four times.

Detach the fish from the skewers when cooked, then separate the fish and bacon. Finely chop the bacon pieces.

Dress the fish in the marinade, season and sprinkle the bacon and Parmesan over the top. Serve warmish.

Chef's tips

This dish is wonderful with the bitter taste of radicchio. Shred two heads and serve the salad on top.

Braised Squid with a Parsley Stuffing

INGREDIENTS *serves 6*
12 squid (about 3¼in long)
2 tbsp finely chopped fresh parsley
2 cloves garlic, crushed
3 tbsp freshly grated Parmesan cheese
½ cup fresh breadcrumbs
2 anchovy fillets
1 egg
6 tbsp olive oil
8oz fresh or canned plum tomatoes
⅔ cup dry white wine
1 chili pepper
salt to taste

PREPARATION
Clean the squid and finely chop the tentacles. (See Chef's Tips.) Combine the parsley, the garlic, and the breadcrumbs. Mash and mix in the anchovy fillets.

Beat the egg and mix it with the bread mixture. Add about half the oil and the tentacles of the squid. Now push the mixture into the squid bodies, stopping about two thirds of the way down. (The squid will shrink as it cooks and thus push the stuffing down to the end.)

Heat the rest of the oil in a pan large enough to hold all the fish in one layer. Roughly chop the tomatoes and add them to the oil with the wine and the whole chili.

Bring the tomatoes and wine to a boil, then turn the heat to a very low simmer. Add the squid and seal the pan tightly. Cook for about 30 minutes, until a fork will easily pierce the squid. Season the sauce and wait, if you like – this dish may be served hot, cold or in between.

Chef's tips

Cleaning squid: seize the tentacles and pull – the head and digestive businesses will follow them easily out of the tube-like outer body. Run your finger down the body to squeeze out any residue.

You will notice the tip of something that looks like a piece of transparent cellulose protruding from the body sac. This is the creature's extraordinary backbone. Thumb and forefinger will tease it out quite easily. But don't snap it: it will become difficult to reach.

Cut the tentacles away just above the point they join. Discard the rest.

Salmon Stuffed with Black Olives

INGREDIENTS *serves 6*

1 small salmon (about 4½lb)
8oz fresh or canned plum tomatoes
4 tbsp olive oil
4 cloves garlic
2 sprigs *fresh* rosemary
6 anchovy fillets
⅓ cup black olives
2 tbsp white wine vinegar
4 tbsp dry white wine
2 tbsp brandy
salt and freshly ground black pepper to taste

Above: Salmon or salmon trout stuffed with black olives

PREPARATION

Preheat the oven to 350°F. Clean and de-scale the fish. (See Chef's Tips on page 175.)

Roughly chop the tomatoes and spread them out on a large sheet of foil. Mix the olive oil with the chopped tomatoes and lay the fish on top.

Crush the garlic and smear the inside of the fish with it; lay the sprigs of rosemary and the anchovy fillets at equal intervals inside the cavity. Chop the olives very finely and sprinkle half inside, half outside.

Combine the wine vinegar and brandy and pour over the fish, then lift the sides of the foil and seal the fish carefully. Bake the fish for 35 minutes.

Lift the fish from the foil with a long fish slice when it is cooked. Take care when transferring it so that it does not break, and set it on a serving dish.

Pour all the juices from the foil into a pan and bring them to a rapid boil. Season with the salt and pepper, pour over the fish and serve immediately.

Red Mullet Livorno Style

INGREDIENTS *serves 4*
1 lb ripe tomatoes
2 tbsp butter
olive oil
few fresh basil leaves, chopped
salt and pepper
4 red mullet
1 stick celery
1 clove garlic
4 tbsp chopped parsley
all-purpose flour

PREPARATION
Wash the tomatoes, peel and press through a strainer. In a small pan, heat the butter, 2 tbsp oil and the basil, then add the tomatoes, season with salt and pepper and cook gently for 30 minutes.

Meanwhile, clean and scale the fish and remove the fins; wash the fish and pat dry. Finely chop the celery and garlic. Place the celery, garlic, parsley and about ¼ cup oil into a pan which you can bring to the table. Fry for a few minutes.

Lightly flour the fish and brown on one side. Remove from the heat and very carefully (mullet are fragile) turn them over. Put them back on the heat. Pour over the tomato sauce and cook for about 10 minutes. Serve the fish in the pan.

Above: Red mullet Livorno style

Italian Grilled Fish

INGREDIENTS *serves 4*
6 whole fish (about 12oz each)
⅔ cup olive oil
juice of 1 lemon
freshly grated black pepper
2 tbsp fresh oregano
1 tbsp very fine breadcrumbs
rock salt to taste

PREPARATION
Clean, dry and de-scale the fish, if necessary. Combine the oil and lemon juice and coat the fish thoroughly.

Combine the black pepper, oregano, breadcrumbs and salt and rub into the fish. Leave for about 2 hours.

Heat the broiler to maximum heat and cook the fish, turning only once.

Chef's tip

Any fish will do, but sea fish are recommended. The crucial quality is *absolute* freshness. Use mackerel only if you caught it yourself.

Red Mullet with Ham

INGREDIENTS *serves 4*

12 small red mullet
salt
12 slices prosciutto
4 ripe tomatoes
1 clove garlic
olive oil
¼ cup breadcrumbs
pepper
1 tbsp chopped parsley
juice of ½ lemon

PREPARATION

Clean and scale the fish; wash, pat dry and season with salt. Wrap each one in a slice of prosciutto. Peel the tomatoes, then seed and slice them.

Cook the garlic for 5 minutes in a pan with some oil. Add the mullet and cook for 2-3 minutes on each side, turning them over gently.

Add the tomatoes, sprinkle with breadcrumbs, season with salt and pepper and cook over low heat for 10 minutes. Sprinkle with parsley and lemon juice. Put the mullet on a dish and serve.

Below: Red mullet with ham

Chef's tips

De-scaling can be a messy process. Flakes fly everywhere. If you can, therefore, hold the fish underwater as you scrape. Hold the knife at right angles to the fish and scrape from tail to head to dislodge the scales.

To clean a fish, make a single cut from the waste pipe to the mouth. Push your hand up into the head, close your fingers firmly and pull. Everything from the lungs down will come away, if not cleanly. Wash away all traces of blood and proceed.

Baked Sea Bass with Mayonnaise

INGREDIENTS *serves 6*

1 sea bass (about 3½lb)
2 large onions
¼ cup olive oil
2 cloves garlic
2 sprigs rosemary
2 tbsp finely chopped fresh parsley
2 tbsp finely chopped fresh basil
juice of 1 lemon
¼ cup dry white wine
salt and freshly ground black pepper
2½ cups (see page 133.)

PREPARATION

Preheat the oven to 350°F .

Clean and de-scale the fish (see Chef's Tips, left).

Very finely slice the onion and make a fish-shaped bed of it on a large piece of foil. Pour the olive oil over it and lay the sea bass on the top.

Now crush the garlic and smear it along the inside of the fish. Lay the sprigs of rosemary in there too. Chop the parsley and basil finely, mix with the lemon juice, and similarly anoint the inside of the fish.

Raise the edges of the foil, pour over the white wine and season. Seal the parcel carefully, making absolutely sure there are no holes or tears.

Set the parcel in an ample-sized dish and bake for 30 minutes. When ready, remove from the oven, but do not unseal until the parcel is completely cool. In the meantime, make the mayonnaise.

About 45 minutes before eating, remove the fish from its wrapper and collect all the juices into a small saucepan. Boil them down and leave to cool; then add them to the mayonnaise.

Decorate the fish with the onions on which it lay and serve.

POULTRY AND GAME

Poultry and game, for Italians who live in the country or in the poorer south, are virtually free foods. Many families have chickens scratching about in their back yards and hunting is a national pastime, be it for pheasant, quail, rabbit, hare or even wild boar.

Chicken Braised with Bacon and Red Peppers

INGREDIENTS *serves 4*

2½-3lb chicken
4 tbsp olive oil
4 red bell peppers
4 cloves garlic
4 chili peppers
½lb bacon *or* pancetta salt to taste

PREPARATION

Joint the chicken into four pieces. Heat the oil in your heaviest casserole – one with a good lid – and thoroughly brown the chicken pieces. Remove them from the heat.

De-seed the red peppers and slice into fine strips. Cook until soft in the chicken oil – about 10 minutes. Return the chicken pieces to the pan, smothering them with the sliced peppers.

Add the whole garlic and the whole chilies. Lay the strips of bacon over everything, cover the pan and cook at a very low heat until the chicken is tender – about 30 minutes.

Season lightly with the salt. (Remember that because the bacon is salty you will only need a little.)

Chef's aside

This is a dish that is remarkably easy to spoil. The whole point of it is that the chicken cooks in its own juices, flavored simply by the peppers. No onion. No other stock. The bacon on top provides the lubrication required. Splendid.

Page 176: Chicken braised with bacon and red peppers

Tuscan Fried Chicken

INGREDIENTS *serves 4*

3½lb chicken
1 large bunch parsley, chopped
juice of 1 lemon
2-3tbsp olive oil
salt and pepper
vegetable oil
all-purpose flour
2 eggs, beaten

PREPARATION

Cut the chicken into equal-sized pieces. Put into a casserole and sprinkle with parsley and lemon juice. Pour over olive oil and season with salt and pepper. Turn the chicken in the marinade and let stand for about 2 hours.

Twenty minutes before you are ready to eat, heat some oil for frying in a large skillet. Remove the chicken from the marinade, dust with flour and coat with beaten egg. When the oil is very hot, add the chicken and fry over medium heat for about 15 minutes or until crisp and golden. Remove the chicken with a slotted spoon and drain on paper towels. Season again with salt and serve very hot.

Italian Broiled Chicken

INGREDIENTS *serves 4*

2½-3lb chicken
juice of two lemons
⅔ cup olive oil
1 heaped tbsp peppercorns
rock salt to taste

PREPARATION

Take a large pair of scissors to the chicken's backbone and cut it out. Lay the bird breast side up on your work-top and press down on to the breast to flatten it. Now cut diagonal slashes across the breasts and thighs.

Set the chicken in a dish and pour over it the lemon juice and olive oil. Very roughly crush the peppercorns and sprinkle them over the chicken. Let it marinade for about two hours.

Preheat the broiler. It should be as hot as possible. Sprinkle the chicken breasts liberally with the rock salt. Broil until the breasts turn light brown. Turn the chicken over. Pour some of the marinade into the cavity and broil on for a further 10 minutes.

Turn once more, baste with the marinade (scoop up the juices from the broiler pan, too), and remove when the whole bird is an appetizing mid-brown.

Italian Roast Chicken with Rosemary

INGREDIENTS *serves 4*

2½-3lb chicken
4 cloves garlic
4 good sprigs fresh rosemary
⅔ cup tritto (see page 183)
4 tbsp olive oil
4 tbsp dry white wine
salt to taste

PREPARATION

Preheat the oven to 375°F. Put the chicken in a roasting pan, crush the garlic roughly and smear it around the cavity of the chicken, and put 2 sprigs of rosemary inside with it, then chop the remainder and sprinkle it over and around the bird with tritto and oil. Commit the whole ensemble to the oven.

The chicken will be cooked in an hour or so, but baste it thoroughly with the pan juices every 15 minutes.

When cooking is complete, let the bird rest for 5 minutes or so. Skim the oil off the pan juices and set the dish over a very hot flame. Add the wine and bring everything to a rapid boil. Season, pour over the chicken and serve immediately.

Chicken Stuffed with Artichokes

INGREDIENTS *serves 4*

1 clove garlic
rosemary sprig
2 tbsp butter
salt and pepper
3lb chicken
4 cooked artichoke hearts
1 lemon, pierced in several places
4 fresh sage leaves
2 tbsp olive oil
about ¾ cup dry white wine

PREPARATION

Preheat the oven to 350°F. Crush the garlic and rosemary. Put in a bowl with the butter, salt and pepper; mix with a wooden spoon until finely creamed.

Wash the chicken, pat dry and stuff with artichokes and lemon. Sew up the opening with cooking thread. Skewer the chicken together with a thin skewer, putting 1 sage leaf under each wing and each leg. Rub the butter mixture all over the chicken, then sprinkle with salt and pepper. Put in a baking pan or dish and pour oil over. Roast for 1½ hours, turning frequently.

Remove from the oven when golden brown. Transfer to a serving plate and cut into pieces. Arrange the artichoke hearts around the chicken. Discard the lemon. Pour the wine into the pan and heat over low heat, stirring to blend wine and dripping. Pour the sauce over the chicken and serve at once while piping hot.

Above: Chicken stuffed with artichokes

Right: Italian broiled chicken

Duck with Anchovies

INGREDIENTS *serves 4*

10 flat anchovy fillets
8 cloves garlic, chopped
1 onion, sliced
1 carrot, sliced
1 stick celery, sliced
few slices fresh ginger root
½ cup pitted green olives
vegetable oil
4lb duck, cut up
salt
chicken stock

PREPARATION

Put the anchovies, garlic, vegetables, ginger and olives into a large saucepan. Coat with a few tbsp oil and fry for five minutes. Add the duck pieces to the pan with very little salt (anchovies are salty) and brown over high heat. Cover and cook over medium heat for 45 minutes, adding a little chicken stock whenever necessary to prevent the duck from drying out.

Below: Duck with anchovies

Chicken and Rice Salad

INGREDIENTS *serves 4*

1 cup cold cooked rice
½ cup sliced cooked chicken
½ cup diced cooked tongue
6 tbsp slivered truffle (optional)
1 tbsp coarsely chopped fresh basil
few tomatoes, sliced
small lettuce leaves
about 3 tbsp vegetable oil
juice of 1 lemon
3 tbsp whipping cream
salt and pepper

PREPARATION

Mix the rice, chicken, tongue and truffle (if used) together in a bowl. Sprinkle with basil and decorate the edges with tomatoes and lettuce. Make the dressing by mixing together oil, lemon juice and cream; season with salt and pepper. Pour over the salad.

Turkey Breast Bologna Style

INGREDIENTS *serves 4*

1¼lb turkey breast, sliced
½ cup butter
all-purpose flour
dry marsala
salt and pepper
about 1 cup beef stock
1 white truffle (optional)
¼ cup grated Parmesan cheese

PREPARATION

Pound the turkey slices flat. Choose a pan large enough to accommodate them in one layer. Heat ¼ cup butter in pan until it browns. Flour the turkey slices and fry quickly on both sides. Sprinkle on a few tbsp marsala, season with salt and pepper and cook until the wine has evaporated. Remove the turkey with a slotted spoon.

Pour half the stock into the pan. Bring to a boil and add the turkey slices, turning to let them absorb flavor. Cook over low heat for a few minutes. If using truffle, wash it in a little white wine, then cut into thin slices.

Preheat the oven to 375F. Put the turkey in a greased baking dish. Add a little stock to the sauce left in the pan and cook over high heat, stirring well to dissolve any sediment left at the bottom. Cover the turkey with truffle slices (if used), sprinkle with Parmesan, top evenly with sauce from the pan, and dot with remaining butter. Cover and put in the oven until the cheese has melted.

Serve with creamed potatoes, asparagus tips, buttered spinach or glazed onions.

Above: Pheasant braised with three alcohols

Pheasant Braised with Three Alcohols

INGREDIENTS *serves 4*

2 pheasants
¼ cup olive oil
1 medium onion, finely sliced
2 cloves garlic
8 sprigs of fresh rosemary
¼ cup Marsala
¼ cup brandy
⅔ cup dry white wine
salt and freshly ground black pepper to taste

PREPARATION

Preheat the oven to 325°F. Cut away the backbones, then slice each bird into two: cut down through the center of the breastbone.

In a tray large enough to hold the halves side by side, heat the oil. Soften in it the finely sliced onion. Throw the garlic cloves in whole.

As the onion cooks, flatten out the pheasants as much as you can, either with the palm of your hand or alternatively with the flat of a cleaver.

Lay the sprigs of rosemary on top of the softened onions then lay the pheasant breasts down on top of that. Cook thus for 2-3 minutes on a high flame.

Take a fork and liberally prick the upper and still uncooked sides of the birds. Mix the Marsala and brandy together and pour an equal amount over each bird. Cover the dish very tightly and place in the oven.

After 1½ hours cooking, turn the birds, scooping all the onion and rosemary you can on to the tops of the breasts. Now add the white wine.

Return once more to the oven and continue cooking until the pheasants are very tender – about 1 hour more.

Season the pan juices at the last minute and pour on top of the birds.

Squab Breasts with Pine Nuts and Lemon

INGREDIENTS *serves 4*

6 young squab (pigeon)
⅓ cup tritto (see page 183)
⅓ cup pine nuts
¼ cup olive oil
juice and rind of 1 lemon
⅔ cup Marsala wine

PREPARATION

Remove the breasts from the squab. Keeping the blade very close to the high-ridged breast bone, a swift stroke of the knife from back to front will have the breast hanging on by the skin only. Cut through the skin.

Brown the tritto in a very large pan. Roughly chop the carcasses. As the tritto browns, add them, cover with water and bring to a boil. Allow to simmer.

In a skillet containing *no* oil, toast the pine nuts until they begin to brown. Remove them from the heat immediately – they will continue to cook a little of their own accord.

Heat the olive oil in a heavy pan and drop in each squab breast. Cook for no more than 10 seconds on each side. The breasts will puff up. Remove the skin then slice each breast through across the horizontal – i.e. flat – plane. Seal the raw sides of each breast for a further 2-3 seconds in the hot oil.

Pour away most of the oil and return the pan to a high heat. Add the lemon juice, rind and the Marsala and reduce until you have a thick syrup, about 5 minutes. Stir in ⅔ cup of the squab broth made from the carcasses and reduce again.

Toss the breasts into the sauce and re-heat for half a minute. Remove the breasts from the pan, pour the sauce over them, and sprinkle the browned pine nuts on top.

Above: Squab breasts with pine nuts and lemon

Opposite page: Rabbit with peppers

Chef's tips

The squab breasts take no time at all to cook. Very hard and very fast is the golden rule here. They will be excessively tender cooked in this fashion.

This recipe also wins you some extra squab stock, with which you can, if you wish, make a pasta sauce. Of course, the smaller squab yield rather less stock.

Tritto

This is a pungent, well-seasoned mixture of vegetables preserved in olive oil, which absorbs the tastes of the ingredients and then permeates and lubricates the meat. Kept sealed and reasonably cool, it will keep indefinitely.

How much you make at any time will really depend on the size of your storage jar, which should be of the spring-loaded storage type or have a screw top. Make as much as possible: you will soon find yourself using it for roasts of all descriptions and not just Italian ones.

Ample instruction is given in the recipes on the use of tritto but the general principle is this: any time you roast or pot-roast meat – and sometimes even fish – spread the tritto over and around the joint. What the tiny, herb-steeped and caramelized vegetables do to the pan juices is amazing. The ingredients listed show only proportions.

INGREDIENTS

1 medium onion
1 carrot
1 clove garlic
½ stick celery
1 bay leaf
1 sprig rosemary
6 fresh sage leaves
enough olive oil to cover when the ingredients are packed

PREPARATION

Very finely dice all the ingredients into ⅛in dice (or use a food grinder or processor). Sift the pieces together so they are thoroughly mixed.

Cover with olive oil. Try not to use for at least 12 hours. (The tritto should be packed quite tightly.)

Roast Pheasant with Grapes and Walnuts

INGREDIENTS *serves 4*

1 pheasant
4 strips pancetta
2lb green grapes
about 1 cup sour cream
12 walnuts, shelled
2 tbsp brandy
salt and pepper
2 tbsp butter

PREPARATION

Wrap the pheasant in pancetta and secure with a thin skewer. Set aside a quarter of the grapes and press the rest through a strainer or purée in a blender. Drain off the juice and reserve it.

Put the pheasant in a pan; add the sour cream, walnuts, brandy, grape juice and a pinch of salt and pepper. Cover and cook over low heat for an hour, stirring frequently.

Preheat the oven to 475°F. Remove the pheasant from the pan and take off the pancetta slices. Line a roasting pan with foil and put the pheasant in it. Roast for 10 minutes or until golden brown.

Meanwhile, remove the walnuts from the pheasant simmering liquid and set aside. Boil the liquid over high heat until reduce to ½ cup. Add the butter and stir until it melts. Put the pheasant on a serving dish and surround with the walnuts and reserved grapes. Pour the boiling sauce over the pheasant and serve at once.

Rabbit with Peppers

INGREDIENTS *serves 4*

1 rabbit, cut up
¼ cup butter
¼ cup vegetable oil
rosemary sprig
1 bay leaf
salt and pepper
chicken stock
4 green bell peppers, seeded, sliced
4 flat anchovy fillets, chopped
2 cloves garlic, crushed
2 tbsp vinegar

PREPARATION

Brown the rabbit pieces in a pan with 2 tbsp butter, 2 tbsp oil, the rosemary and bay leaf. Season with salt and pepper; cook over low heat for 1½ hours, adding stock as necessary to keep the meat moist.

In another saucepan heat the remaining butter and 2 tbsp oil; add the bell peppers, anchovies, garlic and vinegar. Season and cook gently for 20 minutes. Add the pepper sauce to the rabbit, let the flavors mingle for 5 minutes and then serve.

Rabbit with Onions

INGREDIENTS *serves 4*

1 large rabbit (weighing about 2lb)
¼ cup olive oil
3 large onions
6 cloves garlic
6 bay leaves
3 chili peppers
4 good sprigs fresh rosemary
¼ cup brandy
salt and freshly ground black pepper to taste

PREPARATION

Preheat the oven to 350°F. Cut away the legs from the rabbit carcase and joint each one once more at the knee. Cut the saddle into four pieces: haunch, belly and the rib cage, split in two along the breast bone.

Heat the oil over a medium heat and brown the rabbit pieces for 3-4 minutes. Remove them from the pan with a slotted spoon and set aside.

Slice the onions very finely and add them to the rabbit pan. Increase the heat and cook them until they begin to color. Reduce the heat and add the whole garlic, the whole chilies and the whole sprigs of rosemary.

Return the rabbit to the pan and smother with the onions. Cover tightly and put them in the oven.

After about 1 hour, completely turn all the contents, add the brandy and season. Continue cooking until the rabbit is very tender – another 30 minutes or so.

Left: Rabbit with onions

Roast Rabbit with Lamb

INGREDIENTS *serves 8-10*

1 large lamb shoulder (weighing about 4½lb), cut into 8 large bone-in chunks
1 large rabbit, jointed into 8—4 legs with the saddle cut into 4 pieces
1 large onion, sliced
4 cloves garlic, roughly crushed
4 good sprigs rosemary
12 fresh sage leaves
1¼ cups dry white wine
¼ cup Marsala
salt and freshly ground black pepper to taste

PREPARATION

Preheat the oven to 350°F. Heat a baking tray to very hot. Add no oil. Drop in the lamb shoulder. Seal the lamb pieces by sautéeing very fiercely, then lower the heat until a little of the lamb fat begins to run. Remove the lamb and set aside.

Add the jointed rabbit. Seal the rabbit gently for 2-3 minutes. Remove from the baking tray and set aside.

Scorch the onion in what should be a very lightly-greased baking tray. Add the garlic, rosemary, sage and the wines. Bring everything to a boil.

Replace the meat, making sure the pieces alternate with each other: the fat of the lamb must moisten the rabbit during the cooking process and the flavor of the rabbit must permeate the lamb. Season at this point.

Cover and bake in the oven for about 1½ hours until tender.

Chef's aside

This reasonably cunning combination links two meats with very different, but highly complementary, basic qualities. The result is extremely interesting. You could just squeeze by with half a shoulder and half a rabbit if you want to cook for a smaller number but, really, bulk is best: the juices flow faster and stronger.

Rolled and Pot-roast Hare

INGREDIENTS *serves 6-7*

1 large hare
8oz unsmoked bacon *or* pancetta, the fattier the better
2 cloves garlic
1 heaping tbsp crushed fresh rosemary (half the quantity, if using dried)
1 heaping tbsp crushed fresh thyme (half the quantity, if using dried)
1 heaping tbsp crumbled fresh sage (half the quantity, if using dried)
¼ cup olive oil
juice of 1 lemon
8oz tritto (see page 183)
8oz fresh or canned plum tomatoes
½pt dry white wine
salt and freshly ground pepper to taste

PREPARATION

Preheat the oven to 350°F. Remove the hare's legs. Cut through the meat along the line of the bones and remove the bones. Set them aside. Batten each of the legs into a scallop about ½ in thick. (See Battening Meat Italian-style, opposite page.)

When all four leg scallops are nicely flat, arrange them together, with their adjoining edges overlapping slightly, so they form a rough rectangle. (You are going to lay strips of meat along the longer edge of this rectangle and then roll it up, as if you were making a jelly roll.)

Now for the strips of meat. Running along the back of the hare – the saddle – are two thin, round strips of meat (the sirloins) and they stretch from the shoulder blades to the haunch. Run the point of a sharp knife along the top of the saddle, very close to the spine, from front to rear. This will free one sirloin from the back. Push/roll the meat down over the ribs. Cut it free as soon as there is no more meat between the skin and ribs. Pull or cut off the skin and set aside.

Lay the first sirloin along the rectangle of scallops. Do the same with the other sirloin. Lay the bacon in long strips around the sirloins.

Cut free the fillets (the tiny triangular strips of meat on the inner side of the ribs towards the haunch) and slot them into the meat strips wherever they will fit.

Roughly crush the garlic and all the herbs and rub them into the leg meat and sirloins of the hare. Pour over half the olive oil and the lemon juice and complete the filling with half the tritto.

Roll up the outer leg meat so the whole hare now resembles a fat and untidy sausage. Secure it with loops of string.

In as tight-fitting a casserole dish as you can find, brown the tritto in the remaining oil. Add the hare sausage and brown it evenly. Roughly chop the tomatoes and add them and the wine to the dish.

Cover and bake in the oven for about 1½ hours, or until the hare is very tender.

Season the pan juices, carve the roulade and serve the juices spooned over it. You will have first removed all trace of string.

Battening Meat Italian Style

This is a splendid trick. The toughest meat is rendered tender and the least promising cut can be elevated and extended.

PREPARATION

Take the piece of meat to be battened. Needless to say, it should be boneless.

Place it on top of a sheet of plastic wrap on a reasonably sturdy worktop. Place another piece of plastic wrap on top.

Working from one side of the meat to the other, set about it with the handiest blunt instrument. A rolling pin will do, although you can buy fancy, flattened battening devices specifically for the purpose. (You must use plastic wrap. Without it, the meat cannot slide and spread easily.)

The two recipes involving the technique in this book are Scallop with Lemon and Parsley and Rolled and Pot-Roasted Hare. But just think what else you can do:

- Bone a chicken leg and batten it flat. You will have a very large chicken scallop that can be cooked in seconds, either breadcrumbed or sautéed with whatever you fancy.
- *Involtini* – scallops of meat or fish which have been stuffed with a little something, rolled, pinned in position and then poached or fried. You must be a little delicate when you batten fish, however.
- Portions you might never have considered. The two legs and breasts from one chicken will make eight very substantial-looking Milanese-style scallops when breadcrumbed.

Quail with Pancetta

INGREDIENTS *serves 4*
8×4-6oz quail
salt and pepper
8 thin strips bacon
½ cup butter
3 medium potatoes
4 strips lean smoked pancetta, blanched
chicken stock

PREPARATION
Wash the quail, pat dry, sprinkle with salt and pepper and truss each with a skewer. Wrap thin bacon strips around the quail, securing with thread. Melt half the butter in a pan, put in the quail and cook, turning occasionally. Peel the potatoes, cut into strips and fry until browned in the remaining butter with a pinch of salt.

Drain the quail, reserving the juices; remove the skewers, arrange on a dish and garnish with fried potatoes and pancetta. Add a few tbsp stock to the cooking juices from the quail, using a wooden spoon to scrape off browned particles sticking to the bottom of the pan. Heat through, stirring; pour the sauce on to the quail and serve.

Above: Quail in brandy with peas

Quail in Brandy with Peas

INGREDIENTS *serves 4*
8×4-6oz quail
½ cup butter
about ½ cup brandy
½ onion, chopped
1¼ cups shelled fresh peas
chicken stock
salt and freshly ground pepper
8oz prosciutto, cut into strips

PREPARATION
Wash the quail, pat dry and truss each with a skewer. Melt half the butter in a pan, put in the quail and cook briskly for 15 minutes. Moisten with brandy and let this evaporate almost completely. Transfer the quail to a serving dish with the cooking juices, remove the skewers and keep hot.

In a separate pan, fry the onion in the remaining butter, add the peas and a little stock, season with salt and pepper, cover and cook until tender. Just before removing the peas from the heat, add the prosciutto. Garnish the quail with peas and prosciutto and serve immediately.

MEAT

Meat was a luxury in Italy until after the Second World War. The Italians are very fond of suckling pig, lamb and kid roasted on a spit over an open wood fire, but their favorite meat is probably veal. Some say that the word for veal – vitello – even gave the country its name.

Veal Scallop with Lemon and Parsley

INGREDIENTS *serves 4*
2 tbsp olive oil
2 tbsp butter
1 lb veal for scallops
good ½ cup all-purpose flour
juice of 2 lemons
2 tbsp finely chopped fresh parsley
salt and freshly ground black pepper

PREPARATION
Cut the veal into four equal slices and batten into scallops. (See Battening Meat Italian-style on page 186.)

Melt the butter with the oil over a high heat. Dip each scallop into the flour, shake off the excess, and fry rapidly – about 1 minute each side. Set the scallops aside in a warm place.

Over a high heat, add the lemon juice to the pan juices with the parsley. Return the scallops to the pan to warm them through – seconds only, for they are already cooked.

Serve instantly, seasoned to taste.

Genoese Meatballs

INGREDIENTS *serves 4*
1¾ cups cooked veal, ground
3 tbsp fresh breadcrumbs, soaked in stock or milk and squeezed dry
1 clove garlic, crushed
1 bunch parsley, chopped
few fresh marjoram leaves
2 tbsp dried mushrooms, soaked, drained, chopped
2 tbsp grated Parmesan cheese
salt and pepper
ground nutmeg
1 egg, beaten
all-purpose flour
vegetable oil
solid vegetable shortening

PREPARATION
In a bowl, mix the veal, breadcrumbs, garlic, parsley, marjoram, mushrooms and cheese. Season with salt, pepper and nutmeg; blend in the egg, mixing well. Form the mixture into balls, flatten slightly and dip in flour. Brown quickly in plenty of oil and shortening, then reduce the heat and continue to fry until cooked through. Serve hot.

Italian Meat

Vitello is meat from a milk-fed calf slaughtered at three weeks. Vitellone is meat from an older, grass-fed, non-working animal. Beef comes from a working animal, the ox (manzo) and not from the cow (mucca).

Osso Buco

INGREDIENTS *serves 4*
2 tbsp olive oil
8oz tritto (see page 183)
4 veal shin cutlets (each weighing about 6oz)
4 cloves garlic
1¼ cups dry white wine
12oz fresh or canned plum tomatoes, roughly chopped
2 tbsp green olives, pitted and halved
2 fresh bay leaves
1 tbsp finely chopped fresh parsley
¼oz thyme (fresh or dried)
salt and freshly ground black pepper
2 tbsp finely chopped fresh basil

PREPARATION
Preheat the oven to 350°F. Over a medium heat on top of the stove, toss the oil and tritto together until the tritto softens – about 3 minutes.

Increase the flame and add the veal shin cutlets. Seal them well on either side. Now lift out the tritto vegetables and meat with a slotted spoon. Pour off most of the oil.

Replace the ingredients and, over the same high heat, add the wine, the tomatoes, the olives, the bay leaves, the chopped parsley and the thyme.

Bring everything to a rolling boil, then cover well. Bake in the oven for about 1¼ hours until tender.

When the veal is cooked, lift it out and set it in a warm place. Boil the sauce hard to reduce its volume by about one third. Season with the salt and pepper, throw in the fresh basil, pour over the meat and serve.

Page 188: Veal scallop with lemon and parsley

Tuscan Veal with Ham

INGREDIENTS *serves 4*
2lb veal rump roast
salt and pepper
all-purpose flour
3 tbsp butter
vegetable oil
1 onion, chopped
4oz prosciutto, cut into strips
1 cup/250ml/8fl oz dry red wine
2 medium potatoes, boiled, peeled, cut into chunks
1 clove garlic, crushed
grated peel of 1 lemon
ground nutmeg

PREPARATION
Season the meat with salt and pepper and flour lightly. Melt the butter in a heavy saucepan, add a little oil and brown the meat. Stir in the onion and prosciutto, pour in the wine and cook over high heat until the liquid is almost evaporated. Cover the meat with water and continue to cook, turning the meat occasionally. Just before the veal is done, add potatoes and stir in garlic, lemon peel and nutmeg; let flavors mingle. Put the meat on a serving dish, pour over the cooking juices, surround with potatoes and serve immediately.

Above: Tuscan veal with ham

Below: Genoese meatballs

Veal Kidneys with Mushrooms

INGREDIENTS *serves 4*
1 tbsp chopped onion
1 clove garlic, crushed
vegetable oil
4 fresh mushrooms, sliced
salt and pepper
2×8oz veal kidneys, fat and skin removed
¼ cup butter
chopped parsley
2 slices bread

PREPARATION
Fry the onion and garlic in oil, add the mushrooms, season with salt and pepper and cook through over medium heat. In another skillet, sauté the kidneys in half the butter and a few tbsp oil until done. Season, add the mushroom mixture and cook briefly. Put on a serving dish, sprinkle with parsley and garnish with bread cut into triangles and fried in remaining butter and a little oil.

Above: Veal kidneys with mushrooms

Veal Cutlets with Bacon and Cheese

INGREDIENTS *serves 4*
4 veal cutlets
salt
1 egg, beaten
fresh breadcrumbs
5 tbsp butter
1-2 tsp finely chopped fresh rosemary
brandy
4 strips bacon, preferably smoked pancetta
4 slices Fontina cheese

PREPARATION
Preheat the oven to 400°F. Flatten the cutlets slightly. Sprinkle with salt, dip in beaten egg and coat with breadcrumbs, pressing them on firmly. Heat the butter in a pan until foamy and fry the cutlets gently until cooked.

Grease a large casserole dish, lay the cutlets on the bottom and sprinkle with finely chopped rosemary. Sprinkle on a few drops of brandy, then cover each cutlet with one strip of bacon and one slice of Fontina. Bake for a few minutes or until the cheese is partially melted. Serve very hot.

Veal Cutlets with Pecorino

INGREDIENTS *serves 4*
4 veal cutlets
wine vinegar
salt and pepper
3 cloves garlic, crushed
1 bunch parsley, chopped
2 eggs, beaten
5 tbsp grated pecorino cheese
breadcrumbs
vegetable oil

PREPARATION
Flatten the cutlets slightly. Put on a plate, sprinkle on a little vinegar and marinate for an hour or so. Drain, pat dry and season with salt and pepper.

Mix the garlic and parsley into the beaten eggs; mix the pecorino with the breadcrumbs. Dip the cutlets first into the egg, then into the breadcrumb mixture, pressing the coating on firmly. Fry in hot oil until browned and crisp on both sides. Drain on paper towels and serve.

Veal Scallops with Ham

INGREDIENTS *serves 4*
8 veal cutlets
salt and pepper
8 slices of prosciutto
8 fresh sage leaves
all-purpose flour
5 tbsp butter
½ cup dry white wine

PREPARATION
Flatten the veal scallops and sprinkle with salt and pepper. Cover each scallop with a slice of prosciutto and a sage leaf, then fold each one in half and secure with a skewer. Flour lightly.

Heat 4 tbsp in a skillet and fry the veal over medium-high heat until brown all over and cooked through. Remove with a slotted spoon and arrange on a serving dish.

Add the wine to the cooking juices and reduce almost completely. Add the remaining butter and stir until melted; pour the hot sauce over the veal. Serve at once.

Below: Veal escalopes (scallops) with ham

Stuffed Shoulder of Veal

INGREDIENTS *serves 4*
1 small onion, sliced
⅔ cup sliced sausage
5 tbsp butter
¾ cup rice
salt and pepper
5 cups boiling chicken stock
1 bunch parsley, chopped
1 cup dry white wine
¼ cup grated Parmesan cheese
1¾lb shoulder of veal in one piece
rosemary sprig
vegetable oil

PREPARATION
Preheat the oven to 375°F. Fry the onion and sausage in half the butter. Add the rice and season with salt and pepper; then cook, adding the boiling stock gradually and stirring frequently. When the rice is almost tender, add the parsley and half the wine and leave the risotto on the heat until the wine is completely absorbed. Sprinkle on grated Parmesan cheese.

Flatten out the veal, season and spread with risotto. Roll up the meat, insert the rosemary, secure with skewers and put in a pan with the remaining butter and a few tbsp oil. Roast until brown, turning the meat frequently.

After 30 minutes, pour over the remaining wine and roast for 1 hour longer. Remove from the oven, slice the meat and serve immediately.

Above: Pot-roast beef with cinnamon

Beef in Red Wine

INGREDIENTS *serves 4*

6 tbsp vegetable shortening *or* butter
1¾lb beef stew meat
1lb onions, sliced
salt and pepper
1 cup condensed beef bouillon
robust red wine

PREPARATION

Preheat the oven to 375°F. Heat the shortening or butter in a saucepan and brown the meat in it. Remove with a slotted spoon and transfer to a plate. Then add the onions to the pan and cook until very soft but not browned. (Add a little water if necessary.)

When the onions are very soft, arrange in a casserole and put the meat on top. Season with salt and pepper and add the bouillon. Then add just enough wine to cover. Bake until the sauce is well reduced and the meat is tender (about 1 hour) and serve with hot polenta as an accompaniment.

Braised Veal Milan-Style

INGREDIENTS *serves 4*

1 small onion, sliced
¼ cup butter
2 tbsp olive oil
all-purpose flour
about 4lb veal shanks, cut through bone into 2in pieces
1 cup dry white wine
salt and pepper
about 3 tbsp chopped parsley
1 clove garlic, chopped
strip of lemon peel

PREPARATION

In a large pan, cook the onion in half the butter and the oil until softened. Lightly flour the veal, place in the pan and add the wine. When the wine has evaporated, season with salt and pepper and continue to cook gently, adding a little water or stock, if necessary, and not letting the meat stick to the bottom. Add the parsley and garlic to the veal together with the lemon peel when the veal is half cooked. Continue cooking gently until the meat is done.

Heat a serving dish and arrange the veal on it, discarding the lemon peel. Mix the remaining butter into the cooking sauce and pour over the veal. Serve with saffron risotto as an accompaniment.

Pot-Roast Beef with Cinnamon

INGREDIENTS *serves 4*

3 onions, thickly sliced
6 tbsp butter
2 tbsp vegetable oil
1¾lb boneless beef chuck roast
salt and pepper
pinch of ground cinnamon
juice of 1 lemon
1 cup dry white wine
1 bay leaf

PREPARATION

Put the onions into a pan with the butter and oil. Cook over low heat for 5 minutes. Add the meat; sprinkle with salt, pepper and cinnamon. Pour in the lemon juice and wine, add the bay leaf, cover and cook over low heat for 2½ hours, turning the meat every so often.

When the meat is tender, remove from the pan, slice and arrange on a serving dish. Pour over the hot sauce from the pan and serve immediately.

Steak with Anchovies

Above: Steak with anchovies

INGREDIENTS *serves 4*
8 flat anchovy fillets
½ cup butter
pepper
4×4oz tender steaks
salt
½ cup pitted green olives

PREPARATION
Press four anchovy fillets through a strainer and put in a bowl. Roll up the remaining four anchovy fillets; set aside. Add half the butter and a pinch of pepper to the strained anchovies and mix with a wooden spoon to a smooth paste. Shape the mixture into a cylinder and wrap in foil. Place in the refrigerator for 1 hour.

Melt 1 tbsp butter in a pan and add the steaks. Cook over a high heat for 2 minutes on each side. Drain, put on a dish, season with salt and pepper and keep warm.

Add the remaining butter to the cooking juices, stir in the olives and cook gently for 10 minutes, stirring occasionally. Take the anchovy butter from the refrigerator and cut into slices. Put a slice on each steak and top with a rolled anchovy. Garnish with olives, pour over the hot sauce and serve.

Beef Tenderloin with Capers

INGREDIENTS *serves 4*
8×4oz slices beef tenderloin
salt and pepper
all-purpose flour
5 tbsp butter
vegetable oil
¼ cup capers
1 tbsp chopped parsley
2-3 tbsp vinegar
ground nutmeg

PREPARATION
Pound the beef slices lightly so all are the same shape. Sprinkle with salt and pepper; dust lightly with flour. Heat the butter with a little oil in a pan. Brown the meat; then add the capers, parsley and 2 tbsp cold water and cook, stirring frequently.

In a separate pan heat the vinegar with nutmeg over a high heat, pour over the meat and stir again. Serve the meat on a platter, covered with sauce.

Below: Beef Tenderloin with Capers

Steak with Gorgonzola Butter

INGREDIENTS *serves 4*

6 tbsp butter
¼ cup crumbled mild gorgonzola cheese
1tbsp chopped parsley
lemon juice
4×4oz tender steaks
salt and pepper

PREPARATION

Put 4 tbsp butter, the gorgonzola, parsley and a few drops of lemon juice into a bowl and beat with a wooden spoon until the mixture is smooth and creamy. Roll the mixture into a cylinder and wrap in foil. Refrigerate for 1 hour.

Melt the remaining butter in a pan, add the steaks and cook over a high heat for 2 minutes on each side. Drain, season with salt and pepper and put on a serving dish.

Cut the gorgonzola butter into 12 slices and put three slices on each steak. Serve at once while piping hot.

Steak with Ham and Eggs

INGREDIENTS *serves 4*

6 tbsp butter
4×4oz tender steaks
salt and pepper
4 slices prosciutto
4 eggs

PREPARATION

Melt half the butter in a pan and add the steaks. Cook over a high heat for 2 minutes on each side. Drain, season with salt and pepper and keep hot.

Put the remaining butter into the pan and melt it. Add the prosciutto and cook gently for 2 minutes. Break an egg on to each slice of prosciutto and cook until the whites have set. Season the eggs and lift out the prosciutto with a spatula. Top the steaks with prosciutto and eggs and pour over the juices from the pan. Serve at once.

Beef Kabobs with Mushrooms and Prunes

INGREDIENTS *serves 4*

16 prunes
about 1¼lb lean, boneless beef, cut in
12 equal cubes
12 mushroom caps
8 bay leaves
salt and pepper
1 tsp ground thyme
olive oil

PREPARATION

Soak the prunes in lukewarm water for 1 hour, then drain and pit. Preheat the oven to 425°F. Thread the prunes, beef cubes and mushrooms alternately on to four metal skewers. Put a bay leaf at each end of each skewer. Season the kabobs with salt, pepper and thyme and sprinkle with olive oil. Put in an oiled baking dish and bake for 10 minutes, turning and basting with cooking juices. Transfer to a serving dish and serve very hot.

Below: Steak with gorgonzola butter

Fillet of Beef with Orange

INGREDIENTS *serves 4*

1 tbsp olive oil
4 fillet steaks (each weighing about 6oz)
¼ cup marsala
¼ cup red wine
2 Seville oranges
salt and a generous amount of coarsely ground black pepper

PREPARATION

Heat the oil in as heavy a skillet as you have. Brown the steaks for a minute on each side. Retrieve them from the pan and set them aside in a very warm place. (An oven at 275°F would do.) Over a very high heat, add the marsala and red wine to deglaze the pan.

Lower the heat, zest the oranges and add both juice and zest to the pan.

If you prefer your meat medium, return the steaks to the pan and re-heat them as the juices reduce. For rare steaks, cook the wine and juice down to a consistency of light syrup before you return the meat.

To serve, pour the juices over each steak. Arrange the zest in an attractive way on top of the meat. Sprinkle with salt and a generous amount of coarsely ground black pepper before eating.

Above: Fillet of beef with orange

Croquettes with Mozzarella and Lemon

INGREDIENTS *serves 4*
1 lb lean ground beef
5 large slices stale bread, crusts trimmed, soaked in water and queezed dry
3 tbsp chopped parsley
6 tbsp grated Parmesan cheese
salt and pepper
2 eggs, beaten
1 cup diced mozzarella cheese
all-purpose flour
vegetable oil
lemon wedges

PREPARATION
Combine the beef, bread, parsley and Parmesan in a bowl. Season with salt and pepper, then blend in the eggs. Form into four croquettes and press the mozzarella into them; re-shape the croquettes. Roll in flour and fry in plenty of hot oil. Serve with lemon wedges.

Croquettes with Mozzarella and Tomato

INGREDIENTS *serves 4*
1 lb lean ground beef
5 large slices stale bread, crusts trimmed, soaked in water and squeezed dry
4 tbsp chopped parsley
6 tbsp grated Parmesan cheese
salt and pepper
2 eggs, beaten
1 cup diced mozzarella cheese
all-purpose flour
vegetable oil
2 tbsp chopped onion
1 lb tomatoes, peeled, seeded, pressed through a strainer
coarsely chopped fresh basil

PREPARATION
Combine the beef, bread, parsley and Parmesan in a bowl. Season with salt and pepper, then blend in the eggs. Form the mixture into four oblong croquettes and press the mozzarella into them; re-shape the croquettes. Roll in the flour and fry in plenty of hot oil.

Meanwhile, fry the onion in a pan with a few tbsp oil, add the tomatoes, season and cook over a medium heat for about 20 minutes. Arrange the croquettes in the simmering sauce and leave to absorb the flavors, scooping the sauce on top. Garnish with basil.

Top: Croquettes with mozzarella and tomato (top) and with mozzarella and lemon (bottom)

Bottom: Roast lamb with broad (lima) bean sauce

Roast Lamb with Lima Bean Sauce

INGREDIENTS *serves 4*

1 cup cooked fresh lima beans
2 cloves garlic
½ cup grated Parmesan cheese
about ½ cup olive oil
rosemary sprig
4 fresh sage leaves
2lb leg of lamb
salt and pepper

PREPARATION

Preheat the oven to 375°F. Pound the beans to a smooth paste with 1 clove of garlic, cheese and half the oil. Put the other clove of garlic, rosemary, sage and remaining oil into an ovenproof casserole. Cook gently on top of the stove for 5 minutes, add the lamb and brown on all sides. Season with salt and pepper, then roast for 1½ hours, turning and basting the meat occasionally.

When the meat is done, transfer to a serving dish and keep warm. Put the bean purée into the juices in the casserole, stir and heat through. Pour into a sauce boat and serve with the lamb.

Pot-Roasted Lamb with Juniper

INGREDIENTS *serves 4*

1 large shoulder of lamb (weighing about 2lb)
4oz tritto (see page 183)
1¼ cups dry white wine
2 good sprigs fresh rosemary
1tbsp juniper berries
salt and pepper to taste

PREPARATION

Preheat the oven to 350°F. Heat, if available, a flameproof and ovenproof casserole. (Otherwise use a baking tray and cover it with foil later.) Heat over a medium flame without oil.

When the pan is really hot, drop in the lamb shoulder. Singe it for a minute on one side then turn it and do likewise. Remove from the heat.

Now throw in the tritto, the white wine, the rosemary and the juniper berries. Cover well and set to bake. After 1 hour, check the liquid. Top it up to its original volume with water, if necessary.

Thirty minutes before serving, remove the lid. Season the juices with salt and pepper, and carve to serve.

Above: Pot-roasted lamb with juniper

Lamb and Artichoke Casserole

INGREDIENTS *serves 4*

1½lb lean boneless lamb (leg or shoulder), cubed
½ cup butter
vegetable oil
salt and pepper
chicken stock
8 cooked artichoke hearts
½ cup dry white wine
chopped parsley

PREPARATION

Brown the meat in 5 tbsp butter and a little oil, season with salt and pepper and cook over low heat until tender, adding stock as necessary. Cut the artichoke hearts into strips and cook in the remaining butter with a pinch of salt.

Put the lamb on to a dish, add wine to the cooking juices and reduce. Pour on to the lamb, garnish with artichokes, sprinkle with parsley and serve.

Above: Lamb and artichoke casserole

Lamb Cutlets in Mushroom Sauce

INGREDIENTS *serves 4*

For the sauce

½ small onion, chopped
¼ cup butter
⅔ cup fresh mushrooms, sliced
salt and pepper
ground nutmeg
dry white wine
1½ cups condensed chicken stock
1tbsp all-purpose flour
2 egg yolks
about 1 cup top of the half-and-half
squeeze of lemon juice

For the lamb

8 boneless lamb loin chops
½ cup butter
salt
2 eggs, beaten
breadcrumbs
parsley sprigs

PREPARATION

First make the sauce. Fry the onion in 2 tbsp butter, add the mushrooms, season with salt, pepper and nutmeg, moisten with a little white wine and cook, adding ¾ cup stock gradually.

Melt the remaining 2 tbsp butter in a pan, mix in the flour and gradually blend in ½ cup stock. Cook, stirring, until slightly thickened. Beat together the egg yolks and remaining stock; blend the yolk mixture into the mushroom mixture, then stir all into the hot sauce.

Blend in the half-and-half and lemon juice. Adjust the seasoning and stir over low heat until the sauce has thickened. (Do not on any account allow the sauce to boil).

Then cook the cutlets, browning them in ¼ cup butter. Season with salt, remove from the pan and allow to cool. Cover the cutlets completely with egg and breadcrumbs. Heat the remaining butter in the pan and brown the breaded cutlets. Drain, garnish with parsley and serve with hot mushroom sauce.

Baked Country Kabobs with Rice

INGREDIENTS *serves 4*
1lb lean, boneless pork (leg or shoulder)
3 zucchini
1 cup fresh mushrooms
2 firm tomatoes
3 green bell peppers, seeded, cut into slices
salt and pepper
$\frac{1}{4}$ cup all-purpose flour
vegetable oil
1 onion, chopped
1 cup dry white wine
1$\frac{1}{4}$ cups rice

PREPARATION
Cut the pork into chunks. Cut the zucchini, mushrooms and tomatoes into slices. Thread the meat, zucchini, mushrooms, tomatoes and bell peppers alternately on to four wooden skewers. Sprinkle with salt and pepper; flour lightly.

Heat some oil in an ovenproof casserole and lightly brown the kabobs. Add the onion and pour in half the wine. Cover and cook for 10 minutes, without reducing the sauce.

Preheat the oven to 400°F. Spoon the rice around the meat; add the remaining wine and enough water to cover. Bring to a boil. Cover and bake for 20 minutes. Leave to stand for 5 minutes before serving.

Sweet and Sour Lamb

INGREDIENTS *serves 4*
2lb lamb shoulder
2 cloves garlic
fresh rosemary leaves
$\frac{1}{2}$ onion, sliced
vegetable oil
salt and pepper
1lb tomatoes, peeled, seeded, pressed through a strainer
$\frac{1}{2}$ cup wine vinegar
4 tsp sugar

PREPARATION
Wash the lamb, pat dry and stick with slivers of garlic and leaves of rosemary. Fry the onion in a heavy saucepan with a few spoonfuls of oil; then brown the meat, season with salt and pepper and add the tomatoes. Cover and cook for 45 minutes.

Add the vinegar and let some evaporate. Then add the sugar and simmer for 45 minutes longer, adding a few spoonfuls of water or stock as necessary. Serve the meat sliced and well covered with hot sauce.

Below: Baked country kabobs with rice

Pork Pot-Roast in Milk

INGREDIENTS *serves 6*

4 tbsp butter
2lb joint of boned pork, from the loin or leg
2½ cups milk
salt and freshly ground black pepper to taste
8 fresh sage leaves
2 bay leaves

PREPARATION

Preheat the oven to 350°F. Melt the butter over a medium heat on top of the stove in the dish you are going to use for the pork – a casserole dish with a lid if you have one.

When the butter begins to foam, add the joint and brown on all sides. Now slowly pour in the milk. The stream should be slow enough to boil as soon as it hits the pot. Season with the salt and pepper and throw in the sage and bay leaves.

Loosely cover the pot – with its own lid or with baking foil, if you're using a roasting pan – and place it in the oven.

Turn the joint completely at half time – after about 1 hour. Top up the milk at that point if the level is below half.

When the joint is cooked, let it stand for 10 minutes or so before carving. This gives you time to deal with the juices.

If the milk is still creamy and pale, boil it down until it begins to caramelize. If not, immediately add ½ cup or so of water to the pan and de-glaze. (Don't be tempted to use wine or stock here. What you are after is the pure flavor of the pan juices, milk and herbs.)

Carve the meat, spoon the sauce over it and serve immediately.

Calves' Liver with Onion

INGREDIENTS *serves 4*

2 tbsp olive oil
6 medium onions, very finely sliced
2 leaves fresh sage
2lb calves' liver
4 tbsp dry white wine
salt and pepper to taste

PREPARATION

Heat the oil and add the onions. Allow them to cook until they are soft and medium brown in color. Roughly tear up the sage leaves and mix them into the onions when the latter are cooked.

Now remove the onions from the pan with a slotted spoon and reserve.

Slice the liver into thin strips and increase the flame to high. Toss in the liver when the pan is very hot. As soon as each piece is sealed take the liver from the pan (see Chef's Tips) and mix it with the onions.

Return the pan to high heat and deglaze it with the white wine. When all has practically evaporated, return the onions and liver to the pan, re-heat for seconds only, season and serve immediately.

Chef's tips

You are not cooking the liver the first time out because it will continue to cook when it has left the pan. And in any event, this recipe gives you a second crack when you re-heat it. But remember, sliced finely, calves' liver literally cooks in seconds. There is another thing the Italians frequently do with liver: *burro e salvia*. For that, clarify a large knob of butter, toss in the shredded fresh sage leaves and fry the thinly-cut liver for 30 seconds a side and no more in a very hot pan.

Right: Calves' liver with onion

Tripe with Chilies

INGREDIENTS *serves 6*
2lb honeycomb tripe
¼ cup olive oil
4 cloves garlic, chopped
1 medium onion, chopped
1lb fresh or canned plum tomatoes, roughly chopped
⅔ cup dry white wine
⅔ cup dried ceps, washed and dried
4 chili peppers
1 sprig fresh rosemary
2 anchovy fillets
salt and pepper to taste

PREPARATION
Bring 13 cups water to a boil and plunge the tripe into it. Boil for 30 minutes.

As the tripe is cooking, heat the oil, soften the garlic and onions together in it, and add the tomatoes, the wine, the ceps and ⅔ cup water. Bring to a boil.

As the sauce is warming, slice and de-seed 2 chilies. Add all chili pieces, the rosemary and the anchovy fillets to the sauce. When it boils, turn the heat to a very low simmer and cover.

When the tripe has boiled for 30 minutes, remove it and slice very finely. Add it to the sauce and cook until tender enough to cut with a fork – about 1 hour. Season and serve.

Above: Pork chops with olives

Pork Chops with Olives

INGREDIENTS *serves 4*
20 cloves garlic
4 pork chops
vegetable oil
vinegar
rosemary sprig
few fresh sage leaves
salt and pepper
¾ cup large green olives
1 tbsp vegetable shortening
¼ cup Marsala *or* white wine
¼ cup condensed beef bouillon
1 tbsp chopped parsley

PREPARATION
Peel 18 cloves of garlic; cook for 3 minutes in boiling water, then drain. Flatten the chops and insert the remaining garlic, cut into slivers. Prepare a marinade with the oil, a little vinegar, rosemary, sage, salt and pepper. Put the chops in the marinade and let stand for 2 hours, turning occasionally. Drain and pat dry.

Boil the olives in water to cover for 10 minutes, remove from heat and keep hot in the cooking liquid.

Heat the shortening in a pan with 1 tbsp oil and add the chops; brown for 3 minutes on each side. Reduce the heat, add the drained garlic and continue to cook for 12 minutes longer or until the chops are cooked through, turning occasionally.

Put the chops on a plate and pile the garlic and drained olives in the center. Pour the Marsala or wine into the pan juices and reduce slightly; simmer for 5 minutes, then pour the sauce on to the chops. Sprinkle with chopped parsley and serve.

Above: Ham slices with anchovy sauce

Roast Leg of Pork

INGREDIENTS *serves 4*

3lb leg of pork
½ cup olive oil
salt and pepper
¾ cup hot chicken stock
1 tbsp whole cloves
½ cup sugar
3 cups dry white wine
¼ cup vinegar
cornstarch

PREPARATION

Soak the pork in cold water for 2 hours, then drain and pat dry. Preheat the oven to 325°F. Pour the oil into a large casserole. Season the meat with salt and pepper and add to the casserole. Roast for 3 hours, basting occasionally with a little hot stock.

Drain the meat over a plate and skim fat from the drippings. Pour the drippings out of the pan and reserve. With a sharp knife, cut crosses into the rind of the pork leg; put a clove into each cross and sprinkle the surface with sugar. Put the leg back into the roasting pan and return to the oven at 375°F until the sugar caramelizes.

Mix the wine with the vinegar and reserved drippings and pour this mixture over the meat. Cook for 1 hour longer. Transfer the pork to serving dish. Skim the fat from the cooking juices, strain and bring to a boil. Thicken the gravy with cornstarch. Pour it into a sauce boat and serve with the leg of pork.

Ham Slices with Anchovy Sauce

INGREDIENTS *serves 4*

8×3oz slices ham
pepper
all-purpose flour
2 eggs, beaten
few tbsp fresh breadcrumbs
7 tbsp butter
1 small onion, chopped
5 flat anchovy fillets, rinsed well, mashed
1 tbsp capers, chopped
1 tbsp chopped parsley
vinegar
chicken stock

PREPARATION

Flatten the ham slices with a mallet and season with pepper; then dip in flour, egg and breadcrumbs.

Melt 2 tbsp butter in a pan, add the onion and cook over low heat until soft. Add the anchovy fillets, capers, parsley, 1 tbsp flour and a little pepper. Stir over a high heat for a few minutes; stir in 2-3 tbsp vinegar and let evaporate. Add enough stock to give a slightly thickened sauce. Dice 1 tbsp butter and stir into the sauce a piece at a time, making sure that each piece is fully incorporated before adding the next. Keep warm.

In a separate pan, melt the remaining butter; add the breaded ham slices and brown on both sides, then reduce the heat and cook for 10-12 minutes, turning occasionally. Arrange on a serving dish, pour over the sauce and serve accompanied with buttered spinach.

Sweetbreads with White Wine, Rosemary and Peas

INGREDIENTS *serves 4-6*
1 carrot, roughly chopped
1 stick celery, roughly chopped
2 small onions
½ lemon
1½lb sweetbreads
⅓ cup olive oil
1¼ cups dry white wine
12oz shelled peas, fresh or frozen
1 good sprig fresh rosemary
1 chili pepper
salt and freshly ground black pepper to taste

PREPARATION
Bring 9 cups water to a boil and add the roughly chopped carrot and celery, 1 onion and the half lemon. Poach the sweetbreads in the court bouillon for 5 minutes.

Remove the sweetbreads. You will now clearly see the membrane around them. Carefully remove as much of this as you can and then set the sweetbreads aside.

Heat the olive oil over a medium heat. Finely slice the other onion and sauté it in the oil. Add the sweetbreads, sliced into 1in chunks, and brown them over a medium flame with the onions for about 3-4 minutes. Add the white wine, the peas – if using fresh ones – the rosemary and the whole chili. Cover the pot and poach the sweetbreads for 15-20 minutes. Remove the sweetbreads and set them aside.

Over a very high flame, reduce the cooking liquors until there will be just enough left to glaze the sweetbreads. Return them to the pan, with the frozen peas, if used. Season and serve as soon as everything is hot.

Left: Sweetbreads with white wine, rosemary and peas

Breadcrumbed Calves' Brains with Tomato and Basil Dressing

INGREDIENTS *serves 6*
2 calves' brains
juice of lemon
1 medium carrot
½ medium fennel bulb
1 small onion
¼ cup vinegar
6fl oz olive oil
8oz fresh plum tomatoes
1oz fresh basil
salt and freshly ground black pepper to taste
3 cups fine fresh breadcrumbs
1½ tbsp freshly grated Parmesan cheese
2 eggs

PREPARATION
Soak the calves' brains in cold water and lemon juice.

Chop the carrot, fennel and onion roughly, bring 4 cups water to a boil, and add the vegetables and the vinegar.

Drain the brains, peel off any obvious membranous parts, and drop them into the boiling water. Poach at a low simmer for 15 minutes.

As the brains are cooking, divide the oil between two bowls. Skin the tomatoes and chop them roughly and finely chop the basil. Mix the tomatoes, basil, salt and pepper in one bowl of oil, and transfer to a serving dish.

Drain the brains, pat them dry, and set them aside in the refrigerator or another cool place.

Mix the breadcrumbs and the cheese in a shallow dish. Break the eggs and beat them in a shallow bowl.

Slice the brains widthways into ½in rounds, dip each in the egg, shake off any excess, then press each side firmly into the breadcrumbs.

Fry them in the remaining olive oil over medium heat until the breadcrumbs form a crisp crust. Serve with the tomato and basil sauce underneath.

DESSERTS

Cheese and fresh fruit is the traditional Italian dessert for everyday, but on Sundays and special occasions lunch can be rounded off with elaborate concoctions of cream, chocolate and meringue on a sponge base soaked in liqueur. In addition to some of the sumptuous Italian desserts that can be made at home, this section also includes a selection of dessert cookies. These can be eaten in Italy at any time of the day – nibbled with coffee or an early morning glass of wine, or enjoyed after a heavy meal with a warming and syrupy liqueur.

Italian Fruit Salad

INGREDIENTS *serves about 6*

1¼ cups fresh orange juice
zest and juice of 1 lemon
2 apples
2 firm pears
2 firm bananas
1½lb assorted fruit: peaches, apricots, melon, grapes, cherries, mangoes etc
4 tbsp white sugar
¼ cup grappa or Grand Marnier

PREPARATION

Mix the orange juice, lemon juice and zest.

Peel all the fruit save the grapes and cherries. De-seed everything. As each fruit is peeled, chop it to grape size and add it to the fruit juice mixture immediately to stop it discoloring in the air.

Sprinkle the sugar over, pour on the liqueur and chill for at least 4 hours if you can. Stir the mixture - carefully - 2 or 3 times during the chilling process.

Fragolini Fritti (Fried Strawberries)

INGREDIENTS *serves 6*

½ cup all-purpose flour
2 tbsp butter, melted
1 egg
milk
brandy
1lb strawberries
5 tbsp sugar
about ¼ cup maraschino
vegetable oil for deep-frying
¼ cup confectioners' sugar

Page 208: Italian fruit salad

Above: Fried strawberries

PREPARATION

Sift the flour into a bowl and mix in the butter. Add the egg and enough milk and brandy to make a smooth batter. Let stand for an hour.

Trim and wash the strawberries, then spread out on a plate. Sprinkle with the sugar and maraschino and let stand for about 30 minutes. Ten minutes before serving, beat the egg white until stiff and fold into batter.

Dip the strawberries into the batter one by one, coating well, and deep-fry in plenty of oil until golden brown and crisp. Drain on paper towels. Put on a dish, sprinkle with powdered sugar and serve.

Amaretti

INGREDIENTS *makes 30 cookies*

1¼ cups blanched almonds
1¼ cups superfine sugar
pinch of baking powder
4 egg whites
¼-½ tsp almond extract

PREPARATION

Preheat the oven to 275°F. Butter a baking sheet and flour it. Put the almonds and a little sugar in a mortar and pound to a powder. Pour the powder into a bowl with the remaining sugar and baking powder and stir.

Beat the egg whites until stiff; fold in the almond mixture, then the almond extract. Spoon into a pastry bag. Pipe the mixture on to the baking sheet, making small mounds. Bake until well dried out (about 40 minutes) and let cool before serving.

Above: Zabaglione

Chef's aside

With a very good whisk, this dessert is stunningly simple. The caveat is the usual one with eggs and double-boilers: don't let the water boil and overcook the eggs. You can control the process quite finely by lifting the pan in and out of the hot water bath.

Here are some unorthodox variations:

Add the grated zest of an orange to the egg mixture before cooking.

Add a thumb-sized lump of crystalized ginger – very, very finely sliced.

Use port instead of marsala.

Zabaglione can also be a rather classy substitute for cream. With strawberries, for example.

Zabaglione

INGREDIENTS *serves 6*

6 eggs

3/4 cup confectioner's sugar

6 tbsp marsala

PREPARATION

Separate the eggs and yolk. Beat the yolks with the sugar and the wine.

Transfer the bowl containing the egg mixture into a saucepan filled with hot water or pour the egg mixture into the top part of a double boiler.

Begin to beat the egg mixture – a fork will not be good enough. Minimum for manual operation is a good, bendy balloon whisk. Ideal is a hand-held electrical version. As the air is incorporated into the eggs, it will swell from the heat of the water. It will also stiffen as the heat of the water cooks it. Beat until the mixture increases its volume by at least three times and stiffens until it is only just pourable.

Decant into fine, fluted glasses. The perfect example would be Venetian in manufacture and Baroque in conception. Eat with spoons and amaretti cookies – see opposite page.

TIRAMISU

Pick-Me-Up

INGREDIENTS *serves 8*

- 4 eggs
- ~~¼ cup/4 tbsp marsala~~ BRANDY
- ¾ cup ~~confectioner's~~ sugar
- 8oz mascarpone (or cottage cheese, if stuck) x 8oz creamed
- 1¼ cups strong coffee sweetened with ¼ cup white sugar
- 40 sponge finger cookies (about 3in×1in each) 7oz.
- 4oz semi-sweet chocolate

shaved

PREPARATION

Separate the eggs and the yolks. Set aside two whites in another bowl. Combine the yolks, the wine and the sugar and beat them together.

Bring a pan of water to just below boiling, then turn down to simmer and beat the yolk mixture over the water until it begins to swell and thicken. (Use a double-boiler or saucepan, if you have one.) Set the yolk mixture aside.

Whisk the two remaining whites into stiff peaks and fold them into the yolk mixture, then set aside.

Liquidize the cheese in a processor or blender and fold into it the yolk and white mixture. Check the sweetness at this stage and adjust it to taste.

Dip each cookie in the coffee: let it soak well. Arrange a floor of cookies on your dish then spread the cookies with a thin coating of the egg/cheese mixture. Repeat the process until you have used your last layer of egg/cheese.

Run a knife around the edges of your little building to smooth down the sides. Grate the chocolate and sprinkle it over the sides and top. Chill until completely cold and set.

Munchies

INGREDIENTS *makes 8*

- 1½ cups blanched almonds
- ¾ cup all-purpose flour, sifted
- ¾ cup superfine sugar
- 3 egg whites, lightly beaten

PREPARATION

Preheat the oven to 350°F. Chop the almonds. Mix the flour, almonds, sugar and beaten egg whites and knead with your hands until you have a smooth mixture. Grease a baking sheet and heap the mixture on it in small mounds. Bake until golden brown. Allow to cool completely and arrange on a pretty plate, then serve.

Rice Cake

INGREDIENTS *serves about 6*

- 3¼ cups milk
- pinch of salt
- 1 cup white sugar
- zest of 1 lemon
- ⅓ cup Arborio rice
- 5 yolks and 4 whites of eggs
- ⅓ cup almonds
- ⅓ cup pine nuts
- ⅓ cup candied peel
- ¼ cup grappa
- ¼ cup butter, melted

PREPARATION

Preheat the oven to 350°F. Bring the milk, salt, sugar and lemon to a boil on top of the stove and add the rice.

Cook until the rice is completely dissolved. The mixture should have the dense consistency of porridge. Remove it from the heat and let it cool. Beat the eggs until well amalgamated.

Lightly toast the almonds and pine nuts – but remember, they turn very quickly so do not burn them. Stir the toasted nuts, the candied peel and the grappa into the rice mixture, then beat it slowly into the eggs.

Liberally grease with the butter a cake pan large enough to hold all the mixture. Pour it all in. Bake for about 1 hour, or until a knife inserted in the centre comes out clean. Let the cake cool until it is easy to handle, but still warm, and then ease it from its container.

Let it stand, if possible for 24 hours before serving. It will go on improving for a week or so after that.

Above: Sweet baked ravioli

Honeyed Neapolitan Doughnuts

INGREDIENTS *serves 4*

1¼ cups all-purpose flour
3 eggs
½ cup sugar
1½ tbsp butter
grated orange and lemon peel
½ cup candied citrus peel, diced
1 tbsp brandy
salt
milk
vegetable oil for deep frying
¾ cup honey
cake decorations

PREPARATION

Mix the flour with beaten eggs, 1 tbsp sugar, butter, a little orange and lemon peel, 3 tbsp candied citrus peel, brandy and a pinch of salt (add a little milk, if necessary). Shape the dough into a ball, cover and let stand for an hour.

Make thin sticks of dough and deep-fry in hot oil until golden brown. Drain on paper towels. Into a pan (copper, if possible) put the honey, the remaining sugar and a few tbsp water. Bring to a gentle boil and simmer until the syrup turns a yellow color.

Reduce the heat and add the pastries, stirring all the while so that they are covered all over in honey. Remove with a slotted spoon, put on to a wet dish, and mold with your hands into ring doughnut shapes. Sprinkle cake decorations over them and decorate with the remaining candied peel cut into strips.

Sweet Baked Ravioli

INGREDIENTS *serves 6-8*

For the pasta
3¾ cups all-purpose flour
⅔ cup butter
⅔ cup sugar
4 eggs
1oz fresh yeast (1 cake compressed yeast)
½ cup lukewarm milk (95°F)

For the filling
1½ cups whole unpeeled chestnuts
½ cup unsweetened cocoa powder
¼ cup sugar
½ cup chopped almonds
½ cup crushed amaretti cookies
1 cup orange marmalade

PREPARATION

For the pasta, mix together the flour with the butter, sugar, three eggs and the yeast dissolved in lukewarm milk. Knead the dough for 20 minutes, cover and let rise in a warm place for an hour.

For the filling, boil the chestnuts, peel and press through a strainer or purée in a blender. Mix the chestnut purée with the cocoa, sugar, almonds, amaretti and marmalade. Preheat the oven to 350°F.

Roll out the pasta into a thin sheet and cut into circles 2in in diameter. Place some filling on each; fold in half and press the edges to seal. Arrange on a greased baking sheet. Beat the remaining egg; brush over the ravioli. Bake for 20 minutes.

Sweet Rice Croquettes San Giuseppe

INGREDIENTS *serves 4*

½ cup all-purpose flour
2oz fresh yeast (2 cakes compressed yeast)
2½ cups lukewarm milk (95°F)
½ cup rice
1 egg and 2 egg yolks
pinch of salt
¼ cup seedless raisins, chopped
2 tbsp pine nuts
1 tbsp superfine sugar
grated peel of ½ lemon
vegetable oil
confectioner's sugar

PREPARATION

Mix 3 tbsp flour with the crumbled yeast and mix with enough lukewarm milk to form a dough. Knead into a ball and cut a cross on top. Put the dough in a bowl and moisten the top with milk. Cover and let rise in a warm place for 20-30 minutes or until doubled in bulk.

Pour the remaining milk into a pan, bring to a boil, add the rice and cook, uncovered, over medium heat until tender. Pour the rice into a bowl and allow to cool, then add the remaining flour, egg, egg yolks, salt, yeast dough, raisins, pine nuts, sugar and lemon peel. Mix well, adding a few tbsp milk, if necessary.

Heat some oil in a skillet, shape the rice mixture into balls and arrange in the skillet (do not let the croquettes touch each other). Fry until golden brown, drain on paper towels, dust with confectioner's sugar and serve.

Above: Sweet rice croquettes San Giuseppe

Ricotta Fritters

INGREDIENTS *serves 4*

8oz ricotta cheese
all-purpose flour
2 eggs, beaten
vegetable oil
½ cup sugar
pinch of ground cinnamon

PREPARATION

Spread the cheese on a flat plate to make a layer about 1in thick. Cut into 1×2in pieces; roll the pieces in flour and chill for about 1 hour.

Roll again in flour, then in beaten eggs. Fry in a wide skillet with plenty of hot oil. When golden brown, drain, arrange on a serving dish and sprinkle with sugar mixed with cinnamon. Serve hot.

Orange and Grapefruit Salad

INGREDIENTS *serves 4*

2 large oranges
3 large grapefruit
superfine sugar
liqueur

PREPARATION

Peel the oranges and grapefruit and cut off all the white membranes. Cut the fruit crosswise into slices, then cut the slices in half and arrange in a crystal bowl. Pour on the juice left on the cutting board and sprinkle with plenty of sugar and your choice of liqueur. Chill for at least an hour before serving.

Above: Ricotta roll

Below: Orange and grapefruit salad

Ricotta Roll

INGREDIENTS *serves 2-4*

For the pastry
2 cups all-purpose flour
1½ cups butter or vegetable shortening
2 tbsp sugar
2 eggs
pinch of salt
milk

For the filling
1 egg and 3 egg yolks
½ cup superfine sugar
1 tbsp cornstarch
1¼ cups hot milk
¼ tsp vanilla extract
½ cup ricotta cheese, diced
2 tbsp diced candied orange peel
1 egg, beaten (optional)
confectioner's sugar

PREPARATION

Combine the ingredients for the pastry, adding enough milk to give the dough a soft, elastic consistency. Knead well, cover and chill for 30 minutes.

For the filling, beat 1 egg and 3 egg yolks with the sugar, add the cornstarch and gradually mix in the milk and vanilla. Pour into a pan; place over low heat and bring to a boil, stirring constantly. Remove from the heat, allow to cool, and mix in the ricotta and orange peel.

Preheat the oven to 375°F. Roll out the pastry on a floured board, then cut into rectangles. Put the filling on half the rectangles and cover with the remaining rectangles, sealing the edges firmly. Brush with beaten egg, if desired. Arrange on a greased, floured baking sheet and bake until golden brown. Dust with confectioner's sugar.

Sienese Spice Cake

INGREDIENTS *serves 10-12*
1 tbsp coriander seeds
¼ cup unsweetened cocoa powder
2 tbsp ground cinnamon
1 whole nutmeg
3 cinnamon sticks
½ tsp whole cloves
6 whole black peppercorns
2½ cups blanched almonds
½ cup honey
1¼ cups superfine sugar
¼ cup finely chopped walnuts
⅔ cup coarsely chopped candied orange peel
¼ cup coarsely chopped candied lemon peel
2⅔ cups mixed candied fruit, coarsely chopped
⅔ cup all-purpose flour
confectioner's sugar and a pinch of ground cinnamon (optional)

PREPARATION
First prepare two powders. Pound the coriander in a mortar and mix half of it with the cocoa and ground cinnamon. Grate the nutmeg; grind together with the cinnamon sticks, cloves, peppercorns and remaining coriander and set aside.

Preheat the oven to 350°F. Toast the almonds until golden brown. Set aside. Put the honey and sugar in a copper pan over medium heat and stir constantly until the syrup has reached the soft ball stage. Remove from the heat; stir in the almonds, walnuts, orange peel, lemon peel, candied fruit, sifted flour and spice mixtures. Divide the mixture into two portions; spread each portion on a greased baking sheet in a 1in thick circle.

Place a pie plate on each circle and cut around the edges to make them even. Fasten a double thickness of foil around the edges of each circle to keep it in shape on the baking sheet. Bake for 30 minutes. Allow to cool before removing from the baking sheet. Remove the foil with scissors finally, dust with powdered sugar mixed with cinnamon, if desired.

Timbale of Pears in Red Wine

INGREDIENTS *serves 4*
For the filling
1lb pears, peeled, cored
red wine
sugar
1 whole clove
pinch of ground cinnamon

For the pastry
1 cup all-purpose flour
⅔ cup superfine sugar
½ cup yellow cornmeal
⅔ cup butter
pinch of salt
3 egg yolks

PREPARATION
For the filling, cut the pears into chunks and cook until tender in red wine with a little sugar and the spices. Remove the clove; set the pears aside. For the pastry, combine the flour, sugar, cornmeal, butter (except for about 1tbsp), salt and egg yolks, adding a little water, if necessary. Cover and chill for about 1 hour.

Preheat the oven to 375°F. Roll out a little over half the pastry and line a tart pan, fill with the pears. Dot with the reserved butter. Roll out the remaining pastry; make a lattice top and place on the pears. Bake until golden brown.

Spices

Spices have been used in Italian cooking since Roman times and during the Renaissance Venice was at the center of the spice trade between the Far East and Europe.

Nutmeg is used in savory and sweet dishes that contain spinach or ricotta. Cloves are found in the rich panforte of Siena, vanilla sugar in sweet pastries and creams.

Genoese-Style Sponge Cake

INGREDIENTS *serves 4*
½ cup butter
4 eggs
½ cup superfine sugar
¼ tsp vanilla extract *or* grated zest of 1 lemon
1 tbsp rum or cognac
9 tbsp all-purpose flour, sifted

PREPARATION
Grease an 8-10in round cake pan and dust with flour. Cut the butter up and heat until just melted in a small saucepan.

Preheat the oven to 350°F. Break the eggs into a copper saucepan, add the sugar and whisk until blended. Place the pan over low heat or over a larger pan of barely simmering water; whisk until the egg mixture is warm to the touch. Remove from the heat and continue whisking until the mixture has cooled. Add the vanilla or grated lemon peel, rum or cognac, and flour. Mix well, then add the melted butter gradually, not letting it stick to the bottom.

Put the mixture into a cake pan – it should come a little more than halfway up the sides – and bake for about 30 minutes or until the center springs back when touched. Turn out on to a rack to cool. If you want to fill the genoise, prepare it a few days ahead of time, wrapping it in waxed paper.

Above: Sicilian trifle cake

Opposite page: Timbale of pears in red wine

Above: Sicilian cassata

Sicilian Cassata

INGREDIENTS *serves 8-10*
3 cups ricotta cheese
1 tbsp pistachio nuts
⅔ cup semisweet chocolate pieces
¾ cup mixed candied fruit
9×5in loaf gingerbread
1 lb superfine sugar
few drops vanilla extract
pinch of ground cinnamon

For the topping
3 tbsp apricot jam
1 tbsp confectioner's sugar
1¼ cups superfine sugar
1 tbsp corn syrup
orange flower water
1¼ cups mixed candied fruit

PREPARATION
Line a 10in springform pan with waxed paper. Place the ricotta in a bowl and beat until smooth. Blanch and peel the pistachios and pound in a mortar. Chop the chocolate and candied fruit. Cut the gingerbread into slices and line the pan with it, reserving a few slices.

Put the sugar and a few tbsp water in a pan; heat until the sugar has dissolved. To the ricotta, add the dissolved cooled sugar, vanilla, cinnamon, chocolate, candied fruit and pistachios. Put this into pan, cover with the remaining gingerbread slices and then another layer of waxed paper. Push down and chill for a few hours.

Meanwhile, make the topping. Melt the apricot jam, add the confectioner's sugar and stir until dissolved. Remove the pan sides and invert the cake on to a plate; remove the waxed paper. Brush the cake with jam mixture.

Over low heat, melt the superfine sugar and corn syrup, adding a few tbsp of orange flower water. Stir well, then pour on to the middle of the cake and spread all over it with a spatula.

Decorate the cake with candied fruit and let the topping set. Using two spatulas, lift the cake on to a serving dish. This classic topping for cassata is tinged with green from the pounded pistachio nuts and decorated with candied peel.

Cream Sponge Deluxe

INGREDIENTS *serves 8-10*

6 eggs
¾ cup superfine sugar
grated peel of 1 lemon
7 tbsp all-purpose flour
½ cup potato starch

For the filling

4oz semisweet chocolate
¼ cup hazelnuts, toasted, skins rubbed off
¼ cup blanched almonds
6-8 tbsp liqueur
3¾ cups whipping cream
½ tsp vanilla extract
⅔ cup confectioner's sugar
ground sweet chocolate
candied cherries (optional)

PREPARATION

Prepare the cake the day before eating, as it will slice better. Grease and flour a deep 10in round baking pan. Preheat the oven to 375°F. Using an electric mixer, beat the eggs and superfine sugar together until very frothy. Then add the lemon peel and sift in the flour. Fold in the potato starch. Turn into the prepared pan and bake for 40 minutes. Cool on a rack.

Melt the chocolate over low heat. Pour some of the chocolate into a pastry bag fitted with a fine writing tip. Pipe tiny circles of chocolate on to a sheet of waxed paper and let cool until set. Meanwhile, pour the remaining chocolate on to another sheet of waxed paper, spread into a wide, thin sheet and let cool until set but not brittle; then cut into circles with a cookie cutter. Invert the sheet with chocolate cutouts over another sheet of waxed paper, so that the circles fall on to it; reserve the chocolate trimmings.

Finely chop the hazelnuts and almonds; set aside. Cut two waxed paper strips and place in a 1½-2qt mold to make the dessert easier to unmold. Cut the cake in half horizontally; cut each layer in pieces to fit the bottom and sides of the mold. Line the mold with cake; moisten the cake with 4-6 tbsp liqueur of your choice.

Melt the reserved chocolate trimmings. Pour 2¼ cups cream into a bowl and whip. Mix in tiny chocolate drops, almonds, hazelnuts, vanilla, ½ cup confectioner's sugar and 2 tbsp liqueur. Mix well, then pour half into the mold and level off. Add the melted chocolate to the other half, and pour this too into the mold. Cover with a waxed paper circle and push down the mixture with a piece of cardboard. Chill for 4 hours or more.

Invert the sponge on to a piece of waxed paper and remove the paper strips. Dust with the remaining confectioner's sugar. Then place four paper strips, each 1in wide, over the top of the cake, crossing them and tucking the edges underneath the cake. Sift ground chocolate over the spaces and carefully remove the paper.

Put two spatulas underneath the cake and lift it on to a serving dish. Whip the remaining cream and pipe rosettes of cream around and on top of the sponge. Decorate with chocolate circles and candied cherries, if desired, and chill until ready to serve.

Above: Brutti ma buoni

Brutti Ma Buoni (Ugly but Nice!)

INGREDIENTS *makes 50 cookies*

1 cup blanched almonds
3 egg whites
¼ tsp vanilla extract
1 cup confectioner's sugar
ground cinnamon
ground cloves

PREPARATION

Preheat the oven to 300°F. Chop the almonds finely. Beat the egg whites in a bowl until stiff, then fold in the chopped almonds, vanilla and sugar; add cinnamon and cloves to taste. Put walnut-sized pieces of mixture on to a greased and floured baking sheet, spacing the cookies well apart. Bake for 40 minutes. Put on a wire rack to cool and store in an airtight container.

Slavic Fruit Cake

INGREDIENTS *serves 4*

For the pastry

2oz fresh yeast (2 cakes compressed yeast)
salt
½ cup sugar
1¼ cups lukewarm milk (95°F)
5¼ cups self-rising flour
½ cup butter
3 egg yolks
grated peel of 1 lemon

For the filling

¾ cup hazelnuts, toasted, skins rubbed off
1 cup chopped walnuts
½ cup golden raisins
½ cup rum
½ cup butter
1 cup superfine sugar
4 eggs, separated
about 1 cup whipping cream, whipped
grated peel of 1 lemon
pinch of ground cinnamon
1 egg, beaten

PREPARATION

For the pastry, crumble the yeast into a cup, add a pinch of salt, the sugar and lukewarm milk (reserving a few tbsp). Put the flour in a bowl, add the yeast mixture and half the butter and mix well together.

Form the dough into a ball and put into a floured bowl. Cut a cross on the surface, cover the dough and let rise until doubled in bulk. Then add the egg yolks beaten with the reserved milk, the remaining butter cut into pieces and the grated lemon peel. Knead well, cover and let rise again. Then punch down, knead and let rise once more.

For the filling, chop the hazelnuts and mix with the walnuts. Soak the golden raisins in rum. Cream the butter with half the sugar. Beat the egg yolks with the remaining sugar until frothy. Add to the butter-sugar mixture; fold in the whipped cream, lemon peel and cinnamon. Add the drained golden raisins and half the nuts.

Beat the egg whites until stiff and fold in. Roll out the dough on a floured board. Cut into three oblongs, the length of the baking sheet. Spread the filling on to these; sprinkle with the remaining nuts. Roll lengthwise, brush with beaten egg and place on a greased baking sheet. Let rise for 15 minutes, then bake at 375°F for an hour.

Above: Slavic fruit cake

Almonds

Almonds were first brought to Italy by the Arabs and have been an essential ingredient in Italian cakes and pastries ever since.

To peel almonds, plunge them into boiling water. Remove the pan from the heat and leave the almonds in the water until the skins peel off easily. Alternatively, put the almonds in cold water, bring to a boil, drain and peel.

To toast peeled almonds, put them on a baking sheet in a 350°F oven. Turn frequently until they are golden brown.

Salted almonds may be served with drinks. Toast the almonds, dip them in lightly beaten egg white and sprinkle with salt and cayenne, if desired. Return to a low oven to dry.

For sugared almonds, a favorite Italian sweet, shell but do not peel the almonds. Caramelize the same weight of sugar as you have almonds. Coat the almonds in the sugar and allow to set. Repeat the operation twice more, so that you have used three times as much sugar as almonds. Finally, dissolve a little gum arabic in water and dip the almonds in it. Spread them out on a wire mesh and leave to dry.

To grind almonds for use in cakes, puddings and pastries, peel the almonds and dry them in the oven without allowing them to brown. Pound them in a mortar with superfine sugar and sift the resulting powder.

INDEX

Figures in **bold** refer to recipes. Figures in *italics* refer to picture captions